Table of contents

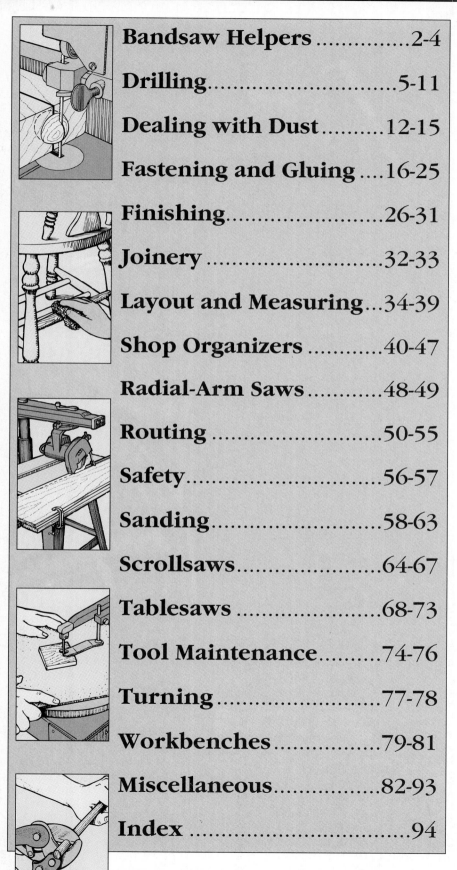
S0-BYW-660

Dear Fellow Woodworker,

Nothing intrigues a good craftsman as much as a new or clever way to do something. That's why *WOOD®* magazine's column TIPS FROM YOUR SHOP (AND OURS) brings in a ton of mail and generates lively discussion and feedback from our readers.

All this information is just too good to keep in the archives. Many readers have asked for a collection of these tips and so here it is—*300 Great Shop Tips, Volume II*—our second book of ideas to improve your shop and woodworking skills.

We selected these tips from *WOOD* magazine issues 36 through 69 and compiled them into 18 chapters so you can locate any subject quickly. On page 94 you'll find a handy index that helps you cross-reference tools, topics, and techniques.

In the old days, skilled craftsmen passed these sorts of tips along to young apprentices, usually with great secrecy. Today, however, woodworking is tremendously popular, and everybody gains when the information is shared. We're proud to share these tips with you, and we hope that they bring you many fine results for years to come.

Sincerely,

Larry Clayton

Larry Clayton
Editor, *WOOD* Magazine

300 Great Shop Tips, Volume II

Editor, Larry Clayton
Project editor: Tom Jackson
Designer: Perry McFarlin
Cover photo: John Hetherington

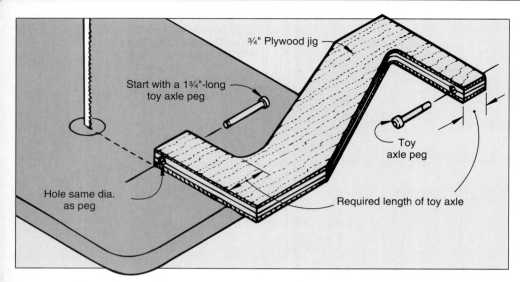

¾" Plywood jig

Start with a 1¾"-long toy axle peg

Toy axle peg

Hole same dia. as peg

Required length of toy axle

Shorten axles easily with a simple saw jig

Shortening toy axle pegs doesn't seem like it should be a troublesome job—until you try to do it. You can't lay the axles on the saw table for a safe cut because of the mushroom-head end, and their small size makes them hard to hang on to.

TIP: Construct the simple jig shown in the drawing. (We show one for trimming two different axle lengths or diameters; you could make a jig with only one notch if you work with only one size.) Slide the peg to be shortened into the appropriate hole, inserting it from the notched side of the jig. Then, holding the peg end against the inside of the notch, cut it flush to the end of the jig with a bandsaw, scrollsaw, or handsaw.

—*David R. McClellan, Markham, Ont.*

Foldaway tabletop extender for bandsaws

Most bandsaws come with small tabletops that don't adequately support large workpieces. You could bolt on an extension table, but what if you work in tight quarters and can't afford the space?

TIP: With ¾" plywood and drop-leaf hardware, you can fashion an extension table. When not needed, the table drops to the side of the bandsaw.

—*Ray W. DeVore, Caledonia, N.Y.*

Toothbrushes can clean more than your teeth

Clean tires on your bandsaw wheels can reduce blade breakage and prevent tracking problems. But, cleaning them is easy to overlook, and as soon as you do clean them, they start getting dusty and gritty again.

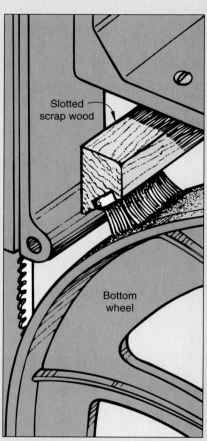

Slotted scrap wood

Bottom wheel

TIP: Mount toothbrushes on brackets to clean the tires constantly. The example shown here is for a 14" Delta machine, but would fit most bandsaws with some modifications. Cut the brush handle short and mount the bristle head in a slotted piece of wood with a screw. Or, you could glue a brush to a metal angle bracket with epoxy. Provide slotted mounting holes or add washers for adjustment.

—*Laszlo Laczko, San Jose, Calif.*

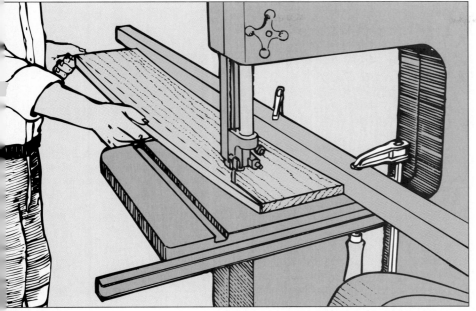

To bandsaw a true edge, set up an extra-long fence

You need to cut a true edge on a board. The only problem is, you don't have a tablesaw or radial-arm saw, only a bandsaw.

TIP: Add a long fence to your bandsaw to true that board. Make one a few inches longer than twice the length of the board you want to true. Clamp it to the saw table, extending a little more than a board length on each side of the blade, and then saw with your widest blade. Cut the second edge against the standard fence.

—Cheryl Diggs,
Virginia Beach, Va.

Undercover magnet reveals tension on bandsaw blade

The blade-tension scale and pointer for your bandsaw are located inside the housing, even though the adjusting knob is outside. So, you must open the housing to re-tension the blade, after loosening it between uses, for instance.

TIP: On a bandsaw with an aluminum wheel housing, eliminate the need to look inside. Just attach magnetic tape to the back of the scale pointer. Place the magnetic side toward the housing, and secure it with tape. Set the tension, using the scale.

Then, move a magnetic stud finder along the outside of the housing until it indicates the location of the magnetic tape. (For accuracy, hold the stud finder so its magnet bar pivots up and down rather than side to side.) Mark that point with paint or an indelible marker. Now, when you're done using the saw, just loosen the blade tension by unscrewing the knob two or three turns. To re-tension the blade, tighten the adjusting knob the same number of turns and verify the setting with the stud finder.

—Earl A. Pyle, Spearfish, S.D.

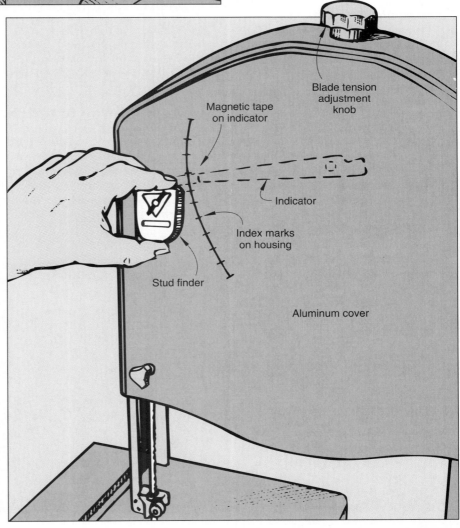

Magnetic tape on indicator

Blade tension adjustment knob

Indicator

Index marks on housing

Stud finder

Aluminum cover

Bandsaw Helpers

Saw a wooden sphere in half with accuracy

Occasionally, a plan calls for sawing a wooden ball in half. Such is the case for a rocking horse that uses two birch half-balls for eyes.

TIP: In one end of a length of a 2×4, bore a hole 1/16" smaller than the diameter of the ball and to a depth that's about three-fourths the diameter of the ball. Also, cut a kerf into the block as shown *below*, centered on the hole for the ball. Force the ball into the hole and cut. (Note: The ball must fit snugly into the jig to give you a safe, accurate cut.)

Afterwards, shut off the saw, allow the blade to stop, and remove the two halves.

—*Henry E. Coleman, Anaheim, Calif.*

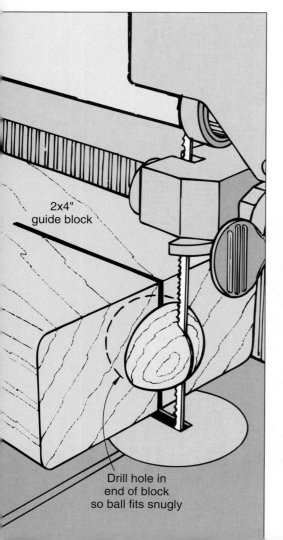

2x4" guide block

Drill hole in end of block so ball fits snugly

Label your bandsaw to save your tires

If you don't use your bandsaw frequently, you should take the tension off the blade between cutting sessions. Leaving the blade tensioned can cause tire damage and tracking problems. But, saws with the tension indicator inside the cover discourage loosening and then re-tensioning the blade.

TIP: Stick a gummed mailing label (or a piece of masking tape) to the tension-knob shaft. Set the tension for the blade you're using and make a mark on the label in line with the saw housing. Now, when you're finished cutting, you can release the tension. When you need to set it again, simply turn the tension knob until the mark on the label aligns with the housing.

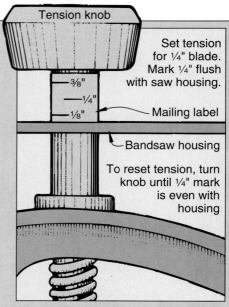

Tension knob

Set tension for 1/4" blade. Mark 1/4" flush with saw housing.

3/8"
1/4"
1/8"

Mailing label

Bandsaw housing

To reset tension, turn knob until 1/4" mark is even with housing

Make separate marks for each blade you use. Whenever you open the cover to change a blade, double-check the marks against the tension scale.

—*Pat McDuffie, Richland, Wash.*

Sign reminds you to retighten a loose blade

You should loosen the tension of your blade when you won't be using your bandsaw for a while. If you do, both the blade and the tires will last longer. Trouble is, you may forget about the loose blade–until you start up the saw.

TIP: Write "BLADE IS LOOSE" in bold letters on a 3×5" piece of stiff cardboard. Then attach a strip of magnetic tape to the card's back. Whenever you loosen the blade, slap the sign onto some conspicuous spot on the saw—the blade guide, for instance.

—*Dick Rentfrow, Raleigh, N.C.*

BLADE IS LOOSE

Dowel provides center for boring bigger holes

You've drilled a ⅜" bolt hole through a project part, and now you want to counterbore it with a larger Forstner-type bit. There just doesn't seem to be an effective way to center the bigger bit on the existing hole.

TIP: Find a piece of ⅜" dowel a few inches long and mark its center. Then, insert it into the ⅜" hole, placing the center-marked end up and flush with the workpiece surface. Now, employing the center-marked dowel as a guide, you won't have any trouble getting that bigger bit started. For a hole of a different size, just use the appropriately sized dowel.

—from the WOOD magazine shop

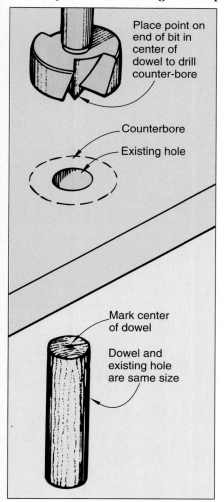

Place point on end of bit in center of dowel to drill counter-bore

Counterbore

Existing hole

Mark center of dowel

Dowel and existing hole are same size

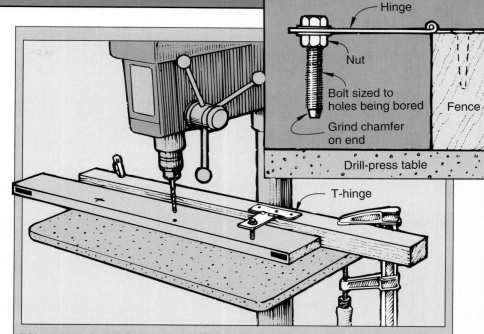

Hinge

Nut

Bolt sized to holes being bored

Grind chamfer on end

Fence

Drill-press table

T-hinge

Hinge swings into action when holes require spacing

Drilling a series of accurately spaced holes can be a grueling task. Even a small misalignment becomes a glaring error in a row of evenly spaced holes.

TIP: Line up those holes smartly with a simple spacing jig for your drill press. Attach a fence (thicker than the material you'll be drilling) to the wooden auxiliary table of your drill press. Drill out the end hinge hole on the long arm of a T-hinge to accept a machine screw the diameter of the hole you'll be drilling.

Now, secure the hinge to the fence top so that the distance from the fence to the screw equals the distance from the edge of the board to the hole location. Clamp the jig to the drill-press table so that the distance from the drill bit to the screw is the same as the space between the holes, and the distance from the drill bit to the fence equals the distance from the edge of the board to the hole.

With the jig in place, measure, mark, and drill the first hole. Now, slide the workpiece along the fence. The screw will fall into the hole to stop the board in position for the next hole. Repeat the process to drill the rest of the holes

—Ed Abrams, Greenville, N.Y.

Rubber tubing eases the grip on chuck keys

Skinny steel chuck-key handles really put a dent in your fingers when you put on the pressure. It would be nice if they were a little fatter and a lot softer.

TIP: From an auto supply store, buy some rubber vacuum- or emissions-control tubing that fits the handles. Lubricate the handles with water or soap, and force a piece of tubing onto each for a more comfortable grip.

—Bill Houghton, Sebastopol, Calif.

Rubber tubing

Drilling

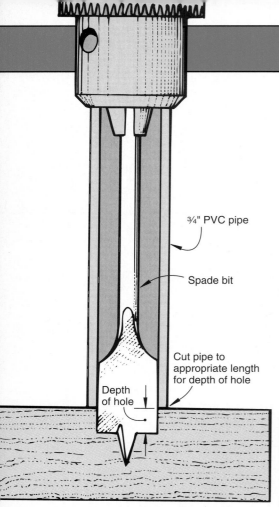

¾" PVC pipe

Spade bit

Cut pipe to appropriate length for depth of hole

Depth of hole

Tape may slip, but pipe keeps on marking

You're drilling a series of holes with a spade bit. It's slow going, though, because the masking tape you wrapped around the bit as a depth gauge keeps coming off.

TIP: Scrounge up a piece of PVC pipe to make a depth gauge that won't fail you. Just draw a line on your bit indicating the hole depth, and then cut a piece of appropriately-sized plastic pipe to fit between that mark and the face of your drill chuck. Slide the pipe over the bit, and drill away. Friction should hold the pipe in place. If not, saw a slit in the end that fits over the bit and place a hose clamp around the end to clamp the pipe.

—*Robert Bourg Jr., Gray, La.*

Make this simple jig for perpendicular holes

Some projects call for you to drill holes perpendicular to a work surface. But, what do you do if the workpiece is too large for your drill-press table, and you don't own a drilling guide for your portable drill?

TIP: Join two blocks of wood at a 90° angle as shown *below.* By holding your drill bit in the corner of this simple jig, you can accurately bore perpendicular holes with many sizes of twist and brad-point bits.

—*Mike Fagan, Elgin, Ore.*

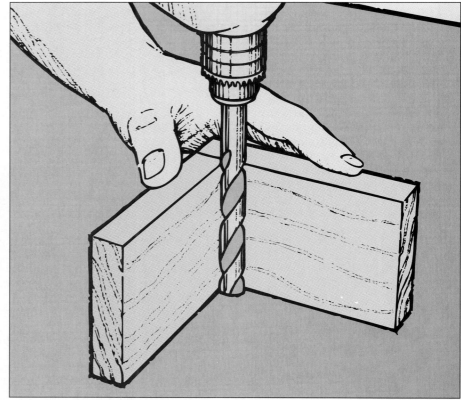

A quick check when sharpening spade bits

You can resharpen spade bits relatively easily, but checking your accuracy can pose problems.

TIP: To make sure that you sharpened both sides of the bit to the same length, just lay the bit into the groove of your combination square's blade. The distances marked by "X" in the drawing at *right* should be equal (1" in this example), with the cutting edges parallel to each other.

—*Ted Wonderly, Mertztown, Pa.*

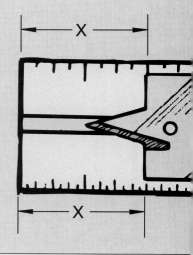

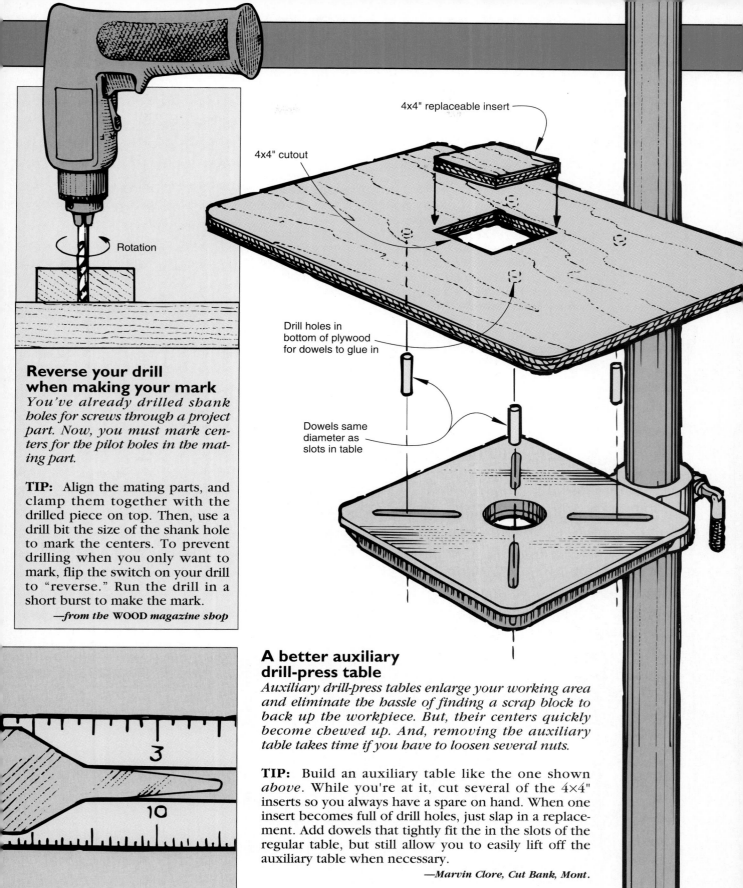

4x4" replaceable insert

4x4" cutout

Drill holes in
bottom of plywood
for dowels to glue in

Dowels same
diameter as
slots in table

Reverse your drill
when making your mark

You've already drilled shank holes for screws through a project part. Now, you must mark centers for the pilot holes in the mating part.

TIP: Align the mating parts, and clamp them together with the drilled piece on top. Then, use a drill bit the size of the shank hole to mark the centers. To prevent drilling when you only want to mark, flip the switch on your drill to "reverse." Run the drill in a short burst to make the mark.

—from the **WOOD** *magazine shop*

Rotation

A better auxiliary
drill-press table

Auxiliary drill-press tables enlarge your working area and eliminate the hassle of finding a scrap block to back up the workpiece. But, their centers quickly become chewed up. And, removing the auxiliary table takes time if you have to loosen several nuts.

TIP: Build an auxiliary table like the one shown *above*. While you're at it, cut several of the 4×4" inserts so you always have a spare on hand. When one insert becomes full of drill holes, just slap in a replacement. Add dowels that tightly fit the in the slots of the regular table, but still allow you to easily lift off the auxiliary table when necessary.

—Marvin Clore, Cut Bank, Mont.

Drilling

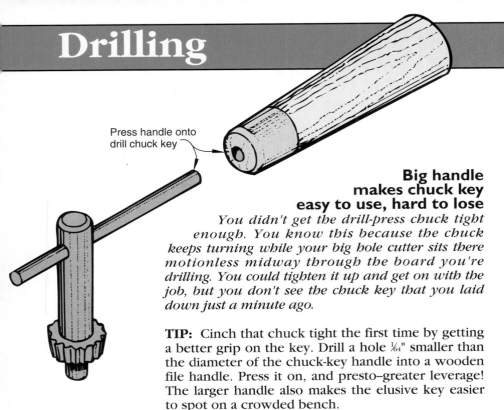

Press handle onto drill chuck key

Big handle makes chuck key easy to use, hard to lose

You didn't get the drill-press chuck tight enough. You know this because the chuck keeps turning while your big hole cutter sits there motionless midway through the board you're drilling. You could tighten it up and get on with the job, but you don't see the chuck key that you laid down just a minute ago.

TIP: Cinch that chuck tight the first time by getting a better grip on the key. Drill a hole 1/64" smaller than the diameter of the chuck-key handle into a wooden file handle. Press it on, and presto–greater leverage! The larger handle also makes the elusive key easier to spot on a crowded bench.

—*Jeff Vanden Boogart, Little Chute, Wis.*

Put an end to loosened drill-press handles

Drill-press handles seem to loosen by themselves. Constantly retightening the handles because of machine vibration can unnerve even the calmest woodworker.

TIP: Remove the handles and wind two revolutions of plumber's teflon tape around the threads. Now, replace each handle and tighten it for a no-slip fit.

—*Dave Godlewski, Sparks, Nev.*

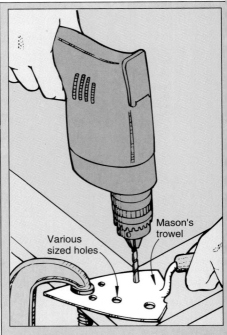

Various sized holes

Mason's trowel

Whip wandering bits with a mason's trowel

Try to bore into metal with a portable drill, and your bit wanders all over, marring your project. Without a drill press, how do you control the bit?

TIP: Make your own drill guide by drilling an assortment of your most commonly used hole sizes in a mason's trowel. To use, start your hole with a metal punch, hold or clamp the trowel flat on the workpiece where needed, insert the bit in the appropriate hole, and drill.

—*George L. Williams, Elk Grove, Calif.*

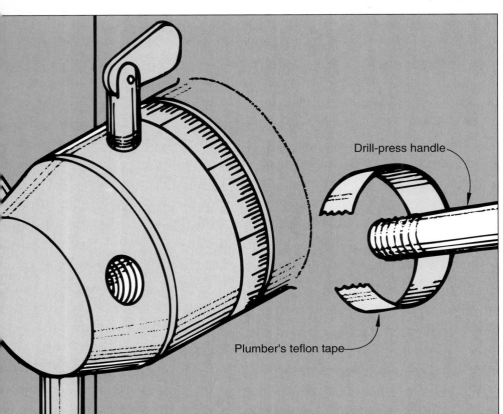

Drill-press handle

Plumber's teflon tape

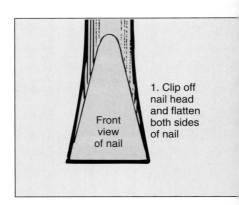

Front view of nail

1. Clip off nail head and flatten both sides of nail

Jig makes for quick adjustment of circle cutter

Circle cutters often require a lot of tricky measuring and trial-and-error adjustments.

TIP: Cut a piece of ¾"×1½" stock to a length equaling the maximum diameter of your circle cutter. Mark a line across the width of the block at its midpoint, and drill a ¼"-deep hole with the pilot of your circle cutter at the center of this line. Then, apply two strips of measuring tape. (You can buy the tape from many hardware stores and catalogs. Apply just one strip if your cutter has only one blade). To get a precise reading of your circle cutter's radius, lower the pilot into its hole and align the cutting point with the desired measurement on the rule.

—from the WOOD magazine shop

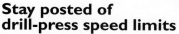

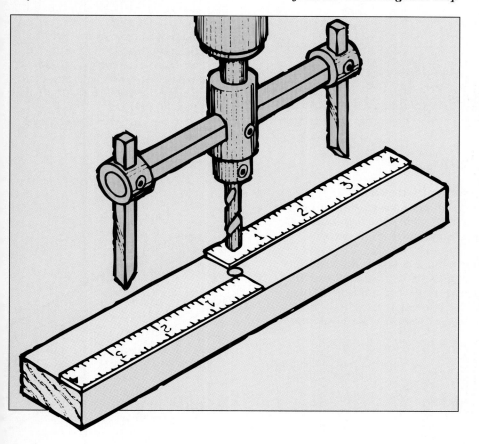

Stay posted of drill-press speed limits

Exceeding correct drill press speeds can quickly overheat an expensive bit, robbing its cutting edge of hardness (temper). The result: dull bits. Slow speeds can lead to poor-quality holes.

TIP: As a reference for recommended rpm, post a drill-press speed chart near your machine (*WOOD* magazine will send you one for $3 ppd.). Then, as an added precaution and convenience, attach a spring-steel letter clip to the hood, as shown *above*, and make a set of cards that lists the possible speeds. Attach the clip with a small screw or epoxy. To show the correct speed setting, display the correct card on top of the stack in the clip.

—Richard H. Dorn, Oelwein, Iowa

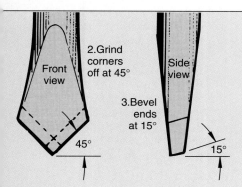

Front view

2. Grind corners off at 45°

45°

Side view

3. Bevel ends at 15°

15°

Turn to hammer and nails when you need a drill bit

You need to drill pilot holes for some screws, but you don't have a twist drill the right size.

TIP: Turn an ordinary nail or brad into a drill bit. Cut the head off and flatten the end with a hammer. When the width matches the hole diameter you need, file or grind the end to a point, as shown at *left*. These shop-made bits work in softwoods or hardwoods, and resist breakage.

—Joe Hess, Calgary, Alta.

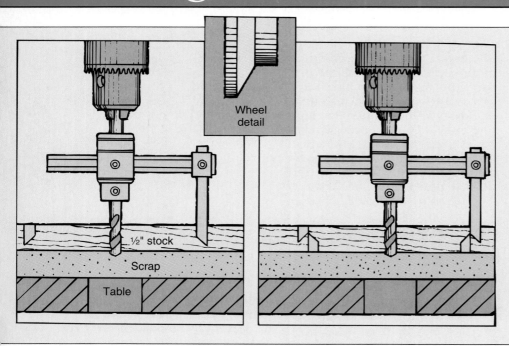

Wheel detail

½" stock

Scrap

Table

Cut out toy train wheels in a snap

Kids love toy trains, but making all the necessary wheels can take considerable time and effort.

TIP: You can turn out train wheels in no time with your circle cutter and this procedure. As shown in the drawings at *left*, cut about two-thirds of the way through a piece of ½"-thick solid stock, and then flip over the workpiece and extend the arm by one cutter width. Now, complete the cut from the opposite face. For consistently shaped wheels, set the depth stop on your drill press for the first cut.

—*Steve Lively, Brainerd, Minn.*

Make these inexpensive, handy hold-downs

When using a drill press, it's crucial to prevent the stock from slipping around, especially as you start the bit into the wood. C-clamps work nicely on longer pieces, but require some setup.

TIP: From ¾" plywood or solid stock, make a few hold-downs as shown *below*. Epoxy wing nuts to lengths of ¼" threaded rod and use ¼" T-nuts on the underside of the table for anchors. These hold-downs also work on other surfaces such as your workbench.

—*Richard S. Mickley, Marysville, Ohio*

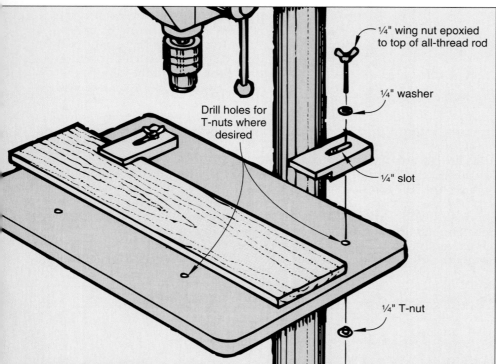

¼" wing nut epoxied to top of all-thread rod

¼" washer

Drill holes for T-nuts where desired

¼" slot

¼" T-nut

Quick reference for hole diameters

How many times have you stared at a drill bit, dowel, bolt, or one of a million other workshop tidbits and tried to guess its diameter?

TIP: Drill holes of graduating sizes, as shown *above*, into a piece of scrap plywood (¼×1½×18" works fine.) Now, you can quickly determine the diameter of all those odds and ends. Don't forget to

10

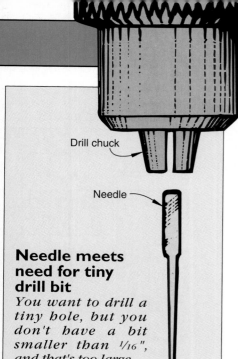

Drill chuck

Needle

Needle meets need for tiny drill bit

You want to drill a tiny hole, but you don't have a bit smaller than 1/16", and that's too large.

TIP: Chuck a sewing-machine needle into your drill to make the tiny hole. You'll find the needles in different sizes and styles at fabric stores or sewing-machine dealers. Choose needles with sharp points instead of blunt or ball-end styles. Look for an enlarged shank, too, to give your chuck a better grip on the needle. Drill slowly to avoid burning.

—Don Greenidge, Floral Park, N.Y.

Eliminate fears when drilling spheres

It's always tricky drilling holes in wooden balls. You just can't quite get a good grip on them with a drill-press vise or clamp.

TIP: Make a simple set of auxiliary jaws that will give a vise or handscrew clamp a firm hold on wooden balls. Just cut two pieces of 3/8"-thick stock (use pine or some other soft-textured wood) to fit your clamp or vise jaws (the ones shown *below* measure 2×4"). Then drill a 3/8" hole through the center of each. Sandwich the ball between the holes, and place the assembly in the vise or clamp for a solid grip. If you have a lot of balls to bore, affix the auxiliary jaws to the clamp or vise with double-faced tape.

—Vincent Ferello, Sarasota, Fla.

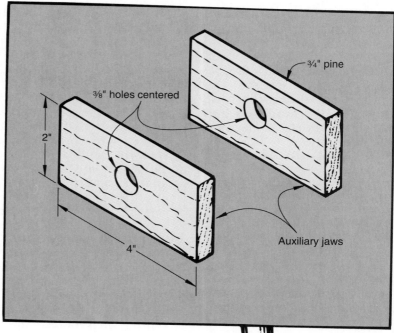

3/4" pine

3/8" holes centered

2"

4"

Auxiliary jaws

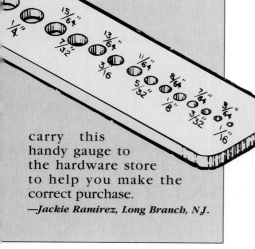

carry this handy gauge to the hardware store to help you make the correct purchase.

—Jackie Ramirez, Long Branch, N.J.

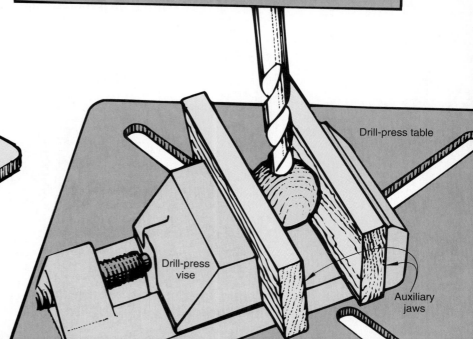

Drill-press table

Drill-press vise

Auxiliary jaws

Big drink cup slurps up the sawdust

You're getting all hot under the collar trying to attach your shop-vac or dust-collector hose to a shop machine. The hose and the machine outlet don't quite mate up, and you're going to have to use a lot of duct tape unless you can find some kind of adapter.

TIP: Relax, go down to the fast-food store and treat yourself to a big orange drink. When you get back home, rinse out the plastic cup and cut the bottom out of it. Now you have a cone-shaped adapter to go between the hose and the machine. The soft plastic cup trims easily, and it's flexible enough to conform to the machine's outlet and the hose end. Fasten the modified cup with duct tape or plastic electrical tape, if necessary.

—*Vence Jelouchan, Florence, S.C.*

Convert pipe couplers into inexpensive blast gates

A built-in dust-collection system requires blast gates. They can become a major expense if you have many outlets in your system, however.

TIP: If you use a PVC pipe for your system, make your own blast gates quickly and economically with a PVC coupling and a piece of sheet metal. Start by cutting a piece of thin sheet metal (you also could use aluminum, plexiglass, or other thin, rigid material) as wide as the coupler's inside diameter and as long as the outside diameter plus 2". This will be your gate.

Stand the coupler on the gate, and trace the inside curve on one end of the gate. Cut the curved end, and file or sand smooth. Bend a 90° angle on the square end, leaving enough lip for a handle.

Next, bandsaw or hacksaw a kerf halfway through the coupling along one side of the inside center ridge. Your gate needs to fit into the slot fairly snugly, so size the kerf accordingly. Slide the gate into the coupling to complete the

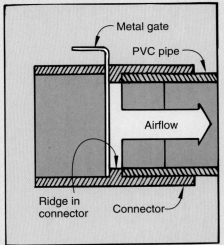

- Metal gate
- PVC pipe
- Airflow
- Ridge in connector
- Connector

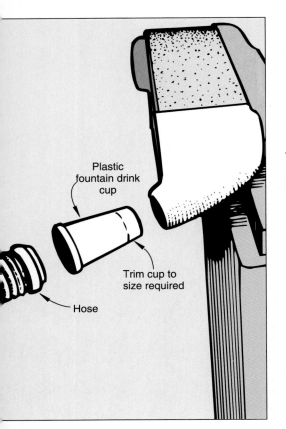

- Plastic fountain drink cup
- Trim cup to size required
- Hose

Hook up a shop vacuum to collect some dust

You don't have a built-in dust-collection system in your shop. Instead, you try to collect dust with your shop vacuum when you're doing a lot of sanding, or routing. You position the hose alongside your work area, but it just won't stay put on its own.

TIP: An S-hook will hold the hose in position for you. Just drill a hole in the side of the hose (or the nozzle) about ½" from the open end. Insert an S-hook (available at hardware stores) in the hole. Then, hold the hose in position by inserting the other end of the hook into a hole drilled in your workbench or tool table.

—*Patrick Smith, Calgary, Alberta*

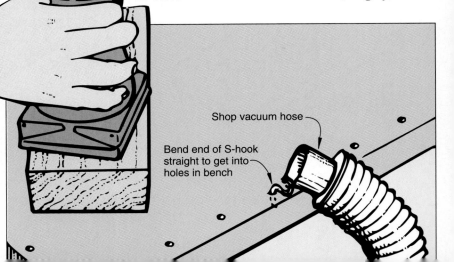

- Shop vacuum hose
- Bend end of S-hook straight to get into holes in bench

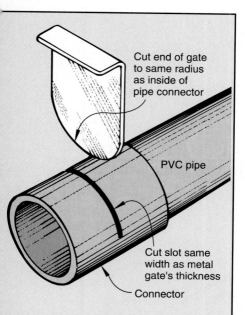

Cut end of gate to same radius as inside of pipe connector

PVC pipe

Cut slot same width as metal gate's thickness

Connector

blast gate. Install it with the longer end of the coupling on the vacuum side of the system. That way, air flow will press the gate against the ridge inside for good sealing.

—*David Weissman, Norwood, N.J.*

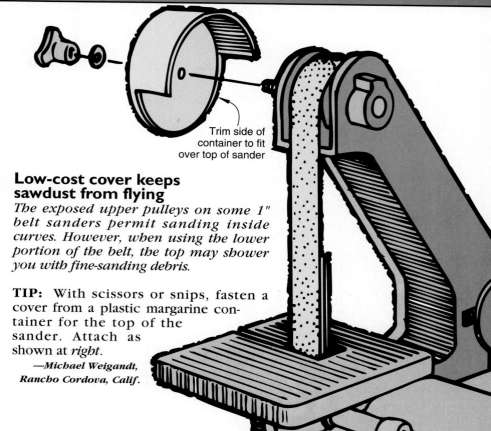

Trim side of container to fit over top of sander

Low-cost cover keeps sawdust from flying

The exposed upper pulleys on some 1" belt sanders permit sanding inside curves. However, when using the lower portion of the belt, the top may shower you with fine-sanding debris.

TIP: With scissors or snips, fasten a cover from a plastic margarine container for the top of the sander. Attach as shown at *right*.

—*Michael Weigandt, Rancho Cordova, Calif.*

Drop box protects dust collector

Ka-chang! There goes another large chip or knot through your dust collector. It sure sounds like it could be doing some damage.

TIP: A simple drop box will catch those large pieces before they reach the dust collector. Build your box to the approximate dimensions shown *right*. Locate the inlet and outlet connectors about 2" above the floor of the box. Make tight joints, and use foam weatherstripping for a gasket on the cleanout cover. Install horizontally near the dust collector.

 Airborne dust passes through to the dust collector, but heavier pieces drop out of the airstream and collect on the bottom of the box. Clean out the box periodically for maximum effectiveness.

—*Bob Colpetzer, Clinton, Tenn.*

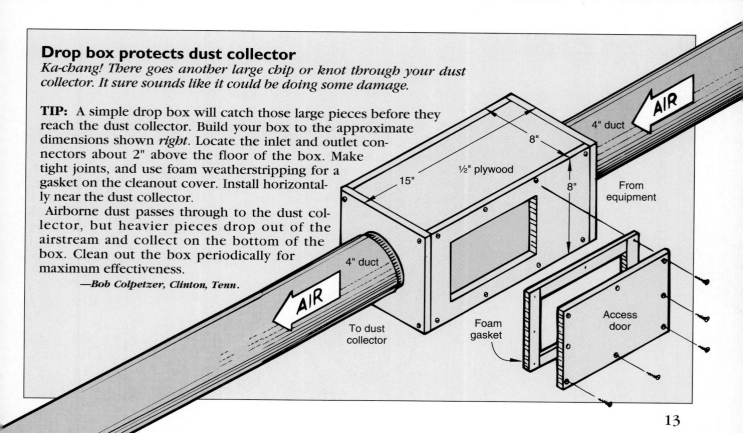

AIR

4" duct

8"

½" plywood

15"

8"

From equipment

4" duct

AIR

To dust collector

Foam gasket

Access door

Filter wrench speeds dust-hose changeovers

Switching your dust-collection hose from one machine to another annoys you. Tightening and loosening the hose clamp with a screwdriver eats up a lot of time.

TIP: Instead of a hose clamp, try a band-type automotive oil-filter wrench. It slides right onto the end of a 3" vacuum hose, and then you can connect or disconnect the hose with just a flip of the wrench handle.

—*Lyman King, Fulton, N.Y.*

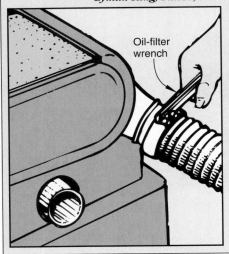

Oil-filter wrench

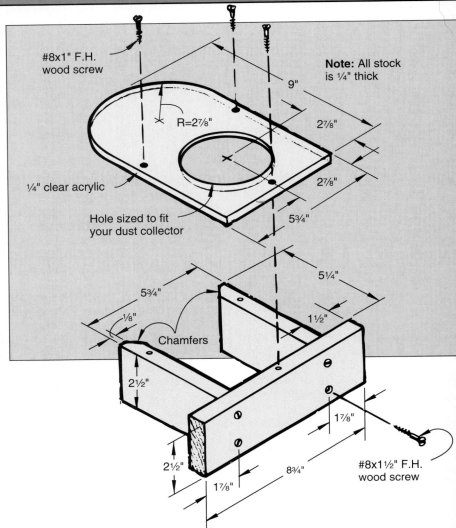

#8x1" F.H. wood screw

Note: All stock is ¼" thick

9"

R=2⅞"

2⅞"

¼" clear acrylic

2⅞"

Hole sized to fit your dust collector

5¾"

5¼"

5¾"

1½"

⅛"

Chamfers

2½"

1⅞"

2½"

1⅞"

8¾"

#8x1½" F.H. wood screw

A dust collector for stationary belt sanders

Stationary belt sanders kick out a lot of sawdust, so it makes good sense to vacuum up as many of the particles directly from the machine as possible. But if you have an older sander, or happen to buy one that doesn't have the proper fittings for dust collection, you can expect big clouds of dust.

TIP: Build a dust-gathering shield from a length of PVC drain pipe and an end cap as shown at *left*. Use a holesaw to bore an opening of the correct diameter to fit the hose of your shop vacuum or dust collector. Mount this collector at the end of the belt and below the platen surface so that you can still sand long boards.

—*William Hurst, Holland, Pa.*

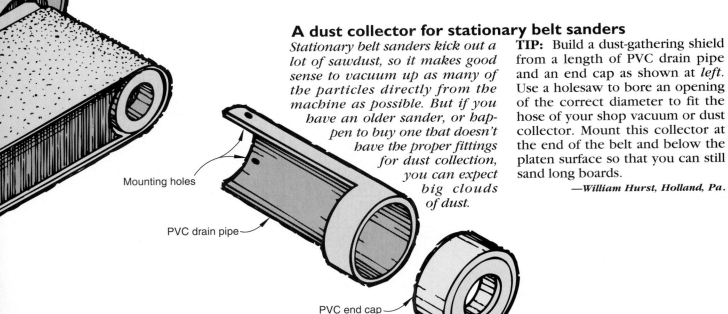

Mounting holes

PVC drain pipe

PVC end cap

A homemade dust collector for your router table

Few workshop tools kick out mounds of wood chips and airborne dust the way a table-mounted router does. It sure would save you cleanup time if you could collect some of that dust at the router.

TIP: Build the simple dust collector shown at *left* from ¼" clear acrylic and ¾" stock. Size the hole to fit your dust-collection hose. Clamp the collector to your router-table fence and plug your dust-collection hose into the hole in the acrylic.

—from the WOOD magazine shop

No more digging in the sawdust

You can lose a lot of nuts, screws, plugs, and small parts when you use a shop vacuum to clean up dust from your benchtop or drawers.

TIP: Cover the end of your shop-vacuum hose with a screen mesh and secure it with duct tape or a rubber band. Choose a mesh size large enough so that it won't clog up, but small enough to hold back the items you want to keep. When you turn on the vacuum, dust passes through the mesh, but nuts, bolts, and small items stop at the screen where you can brush them off easily.

—Jerry Roy, Vinemont, Ala.

Piping for your shop vacuum makes cleaning up a cinch

A shop vacuum sure expedites cleanup, but moving the machine around in a crowded shop soon becomes bothersome

TIP: Place the vacuum in an out-of-the-way spot, such as a corner, and then fabricate remote vacuum-hose hookups with PVC plastic pipe as shown *below*. Select a pipe diameter that matches the hose connection on your machine (1½" works for many). Install T-fittings to provide hose-connection ports, covering unused ones with slip-on pipe caps. Use sheet-metal screws rather than glue at the joints so you can open up the system in case you need to

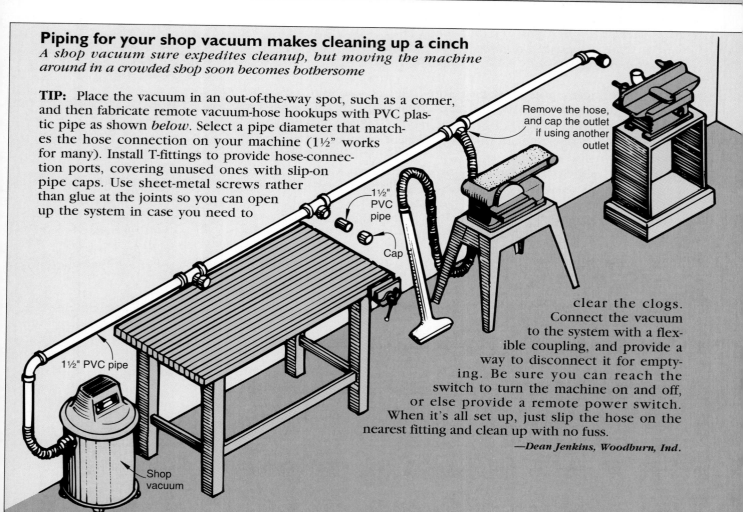

Remove the hose, and cap the outlet if using another outlet

1½" PVC pipe

Cap

1½" PVC pipe

Shop vacuum

clear the clogs. Connect the vacuum to the system with a flexible coupling, and provide a way to disconnect it for emptying. Be sure you can reach the switch to turn the machine on and off, or else provide a remote power switch. When it's all set up, just slip the hose on the nearest fitting and clean up with no fuss.

—Dean Jenkins, Woodburn, Ind.

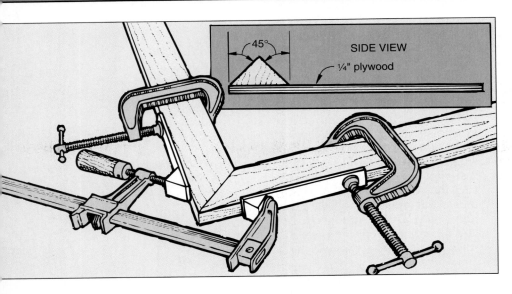

SIDE VIEW
45°
¼" plywood

Beefy clamping jigs strengthen mitered corners

Many corner clamps fail to provide adequate pressure. As a result, the mitered joints are weak or have sloppy glue lines.

TIP: Construct one or more pairs of clamping jigs, as shown at *left*, using 4–5" lengths of ¼" plywood ¾" wide. With your tablesaw miter gauge set to 45°, cut triangular blocks from ¾" stock. Glue the blocks to the plywood strips and, when dry, clamp frame corners as shown.

—*John Tanzini, Hamilton Square, N.J.*

Quick clamping jig makes fuss-free frame corners

Assembling a frame from mitered, rabbeted moldings can drive many a woodworker to distraction. And the project can really go haywire when you try to reinforce the corners by hammering in small brads or nails.

TIP: Bring those corners under control with the easy-to-make jig, shown *below*. On a square of ¾" plywood that is smaller than the narrowest inside dimension of your frame, rabbet two adjacent edges to mate with the frame molding, as shown. Then, cut a 2"-diameter opening 1"

in from each rabbeted edge, 2" from the corner. Cut off the corner where the rabbeted edges meet; then you won't glue the frame to the jig. Attach a cleat to the bottom of the jig so you can hold it in your vise.

To assemble a frame corner, apply glue to the mitered ends, and then place the moldings on the rabbeted edges of the fixture. Bring them together at the corner and clamp each side, placing the fixed end of the C-clamp in the hole. With the pieces held firmly, you can even drive in brads.

—*Joe B. Godfrey, M.D., Forest City, N.C.*

Stock being clamped

Clamp gets grip on longer work

Every once in a while, you run across a project that calls for a clamp longer than any in your shop. You figure it's time to go buy longer pieces of pipe.

TIP: Instead of running to the plumbing shop, go to your scrapwood bin. Clamp short pieces of scrapwood across the over-long part as shown *above*. Then, clamp the joint with one jaw pulling against the scrapwood and the other against the opposite side of the joint.

—*Jim Morgan, Lafayette, Tenn.*

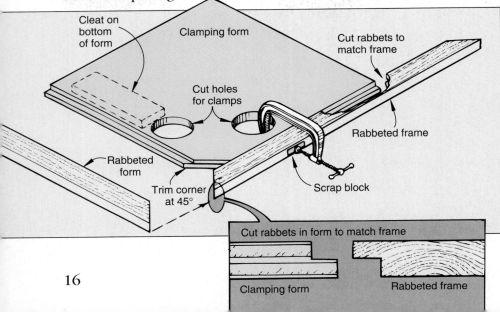

Cleat on bottom of form

Clamping form

Cut rabbets to match frame

Cut holes for clamps

Rabbeted frame

Rabbeted form

Trim corner at 45°

Scrap block

Cut rabbets in form to match frame

Clamping form

Rabbeted frame

Homemade fixtures make diagonal clamping easy

When gluing up the ends of rectangular projects, placing a bar or pipe clamp across opposite corners assures everything will be square after the glue sets—providing you keep the clamp from sliding off the corners. Besides, metal clamp jaws can easily mar or dent the workpiece.

TIP: From ¾" plywood, make a pair or more of swiveling fixtures as shown *below*. Use dimensions that fit your projects and clamps. These fixtures work well without slipping or disfiguring the work.

—*R. B. Morris, Louisville, Ky.*

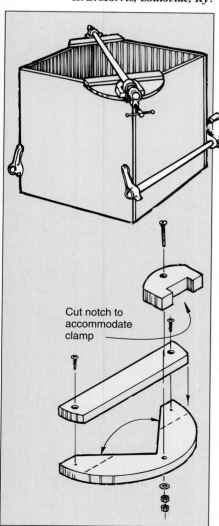

Cut notch to accommodate clamp

Drywall screws can ease your clamp shortage

You're laminating stock to be cut into project parts. But, you don't have enough clamps to flatten the workpieces.

TIP: Before you start laminating, transfer your pattern to the top layer. Apply the glue and build the sandwich as usual. Then, instead of clamping it, fasten it together with drywall screws driven into waste areas.

—*John J. Wells, Defiance, Iowa*

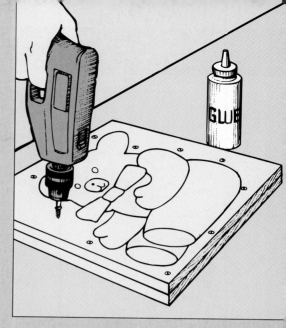

Notched bench dogs bite into round work

Bench dogs are great for holding straight-sided work, but they tend to lose their grip when faced with curved surfaces.

TIP: Cut shallow V notches on one edge of your bench dogs, as shown in the drawing at *right*. These extra contact points will grip irregularly-shaped workpieces much better, including those hard-to-hold curved and circular shapes.

—*Billy Gene DeSoto, New Iberia, La.*

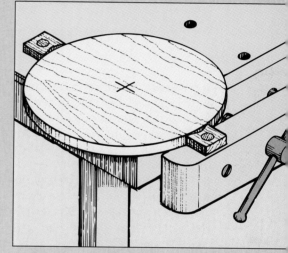

Strap-clamp pointer

Strap clamps often exert more pressure near their ratcheting mechanisms than in the middle of the straps. This uneven pressure can contribute to weak glue joints particularly on many-sided projects.

TIP: You can distribute that pressure more evenly by positioning the clamps opposite each other, as shown in the drawing at *right*.

—*from the WOOD magazine shop*

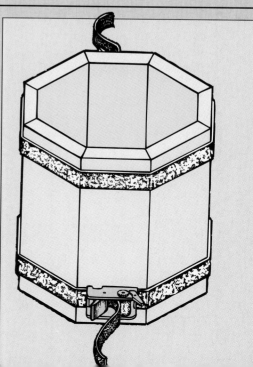

Start with steel to keep brass screws from breaking

Small brass screws often break as you try to drive them in. You really have a problem when the screws are smaller than your smallest drill bit and you can't drill a pilot hole.

TIP: Before trying the brass screw, drive in a steel screw the same size. The stronger steel one will form threads in the wood so your brass screws will go in without fuss or breakage. If you can't drill a pilot hole, poke one with a small wire brad or nail.

—*Lt. Col. D. W. Porter, Woodbridge, Va.*

Elevated pipe clamps

Pipe clamps work great for edge-gluing cutting boards, tabletops, and the like, but it can be a chore to keep them from rolling on their sides as you work. And, elevating the clamps off the bench makes the job easier.

TIP: Assemble two pair of pipe-clamp holders from ¾" pipe and fittings such as the pair shown *above*. First, mount 6" nipples to ¾×6×6" plywood bases with flanges. For each pair, cut one T-joint in half, and drill and tap the other for a ¼" thumb screw. It

Turn your Workmate into a framing clamp

Black and Decker Workmates are just about the handiest shop accessory to come along since the sawhorse, but they do have their limitations. For example, the mechanism exerts clamping pressure in only two directions, so you still need pipe or barclamps when clamping four-sided projects like picture frames.

shaped workpieces with your Workmate. Size the dowel to fit the dog holes in your Workmate, and cut the threaded rod to a length that suits your needs (6–8" should do it). Note that you must flatten the end of the rod before adding the clamp block so the block doesn't fall off.

—*Lyle Kruger, Effingham, Ill.*

TIP: By fashioning four of the add-on blocks shown *below*, you can clamp frames and some odd-

Paper slips glue into tight spot

Veneer edging has a habit of popping loose. The only answer is to deposit some glue behind it and stick it down again. But some edging isn't very flexible, and you run the risk of breaking off a piece if you try to bend it far enough to get your glue-bottle tip in.

TIP: Fold a piece of notepaper in half and give it a sharp crease. Put a few drops of glue into the crease near one end, and slide that end in behind the loose veneer. Now, you can squeeze the glue out of the paper as you press the veneer back into place. You'll have your edge back on without getting glue all over or breaking the band.

—*Brian Breshears, Kent, Wash.*

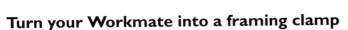

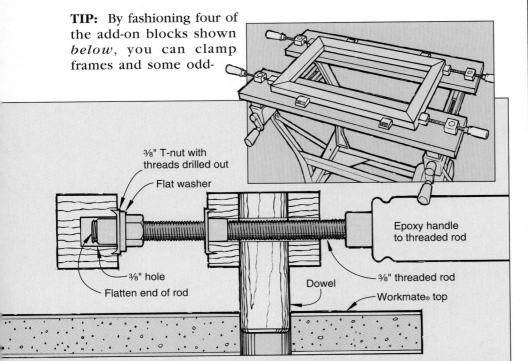

⅜" T-nut with threads drilled out

Flat washer

⅜" hole

Flatten end of rod

Dowel

Epoxy handle to threaded rod

⅜" threaded rod

Workmate® top

helps to cover the pipe clamps with masking tape for protection from glue drips. Once the assembly dries, you can remove it from the holders and replace it with two more pipe clamps for your next assembly.

—*Burl Rice, Topeka, Kan.*

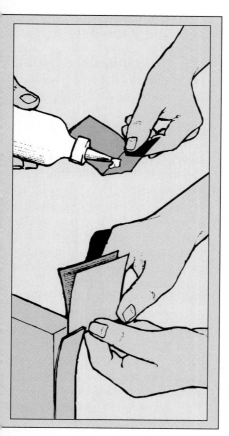

Use one fastener to lock another in place

A lockwasher keeps a roundhead screw from working loose. But, what can you do to keep a flathead screw tight in a countersunk hole, as on a hinge?

TIP: After you've tightened the screw, drill a small hole through one end of the slot in the screw head and on through the piece of hardware. Drive a wire brad or small nail into the hole. This keeps the screw from turning, so it can't work loose.

—*George H. Swisher, Bowie, Md.*

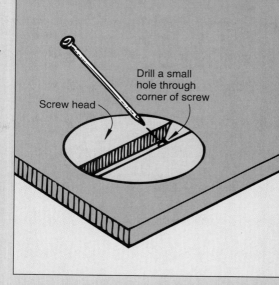

Screw head

Drill a small hole through corner of screw

Cargo tie-down strap cuts clamping costs

Those nylon-strap woodworking clamps are handy around the shop. But what can you do if your tool budget doesn't allow for enough of them?

TIP: Check into ratcheting cargo tie-down straps, the small ones about an inch wide made to secure loads in a pickup truck. Buy them at auto-supply stores, discount stores, or hardware stores. They're usually cheaper than similar woodworking clamps (sometimes nearly half the price) and are more likely to be on sale. There's a drawback for some applications: tie-downs don't come with 90° corner brackets for clamping frames and boxes as the woodworking clamps do.

—*Richard Holmquist,*
Grand Island, Neb.

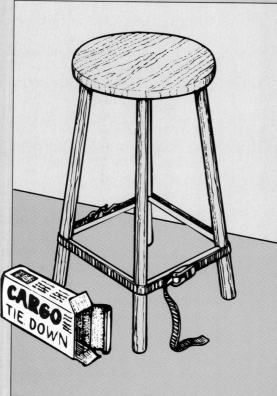

CARGO TIE DOWN

Make those handscrew clamps work harder

Few clamps have the versatility of handscrews, but even these helpers will not apply pressure more than a few inches over the edge of your workpieces.

TIP: Cut ⅜"-deep recesses into two 2×2×12" hardwood blocks. Now, use these blocks to extend the reach of your handscrews.

—*Lee Maughan, Panaca, Nev.*

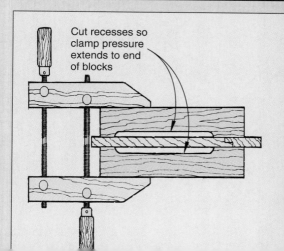

Cut recesses so clamp pressure extends to end of blocks

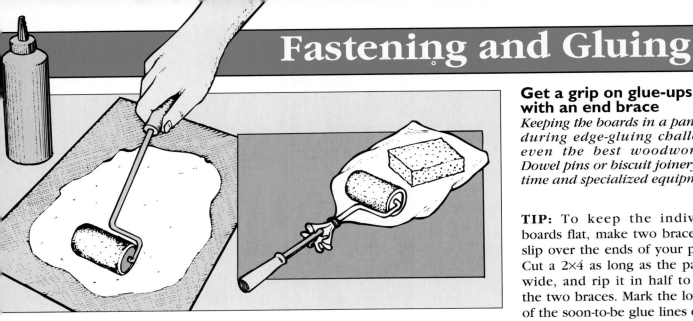

Get a grip on glue-ups with an end brace

Keeping the boards in a panel flat during edge-gluing challenges even the best woodworkers. Dowel pins or biscuit joinery take time and specialized equipment.

TIP: To keep the individual boards flat, make two braces that slip over the ends of your panels. Cut a 2×4 as long as the panel is wide, and rip it in half to make the two braces. Mark the location of the soon-to-be glue lines on the braces, and bore holes at those locations with a Forstner or spade bit as shown in the illustration, *above right*. Next, cut a dado about ¾" deep along the length of

Roll on the glue for better coverage

When laminating or edge-gluing stock, you often need to put on a lot of glue quickly and evenly. Spreaders or your fingers aren't always the best solution.

TIP: Glide the glue on with a 3" paint roller. Just pour some glue on a 10–12" square of any non-porous material. Now, load the roller as you would with paint. When you take a break, seal the roller in a plastic bag along with a wet sponge to keep it from drying out. When you're finished, wipe the palette clean, or scrape off the glue after it dries.

—*Craig Carlson-Stevermer,
Arden Hills, Minn.*

Scrap plastic laminate solves sticky problem

You're clamping boards across edge-glued stock to keep it flat. But, you don't have enough hands to hold them, tighten the clamps, and slip in waxed paper to keep the boards from becoming a permanent part of your project.

TIP: You can save the waxed paper for wrapping sandwiches if, instead, you cement scraps of plastic laminate to the inside surfaces of your alignment boards. Both setup and cleanup will be easier and faster.

—*Dan Campbell, Meyersville, N.J.*

Trick ropin' saves the day when the gluing gets tough

You can fiddle a lot of time away trying to clamp hexagons, octagons, or any of the other polygons you might build. A strap-type clamp is the easiest way to hold them for gluing, but what do you do if you don't have one?

TIP: Get a rope. Then drill two holes (rope diameter) through two pieces of scrapwood near the ends. Thread the rope (sash cord works great) through the wood, as shown at *right*, and tie a knot in each end. Drill a dowel hole on an edge at one end of one piece and glue in a dowel, leaving about two rope diameters of it above the surface. Now, to clamp your work, place the wooden pieces three or four thicknesses apart and cinch the rope around the work, taking in the slack at the end near the dowel. When the rope is tight, pass its end around the dowel and back under itself

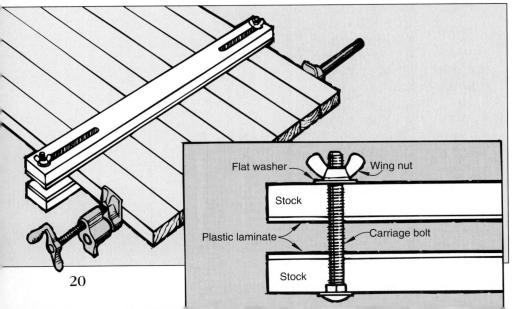

Flat washer — Wing nut

Stock

Plastic laminate —

Carriage bolt

Stock

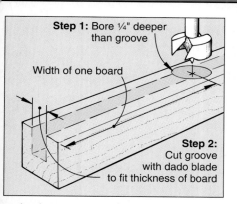

Step 1: Bore ¼" deeper than groove

Width of one board

Step 2: Cut groove with dado blade to fit thickness of board

the braces as wide as your panel is thick. Glue and clamp the panel, and slip the two braces over the ends, centering the gluelines on the holes. The holes prevent the glue squeeze-out from attaching the brace to the panel.

—*Allen L. Formby, Springhill, La.*

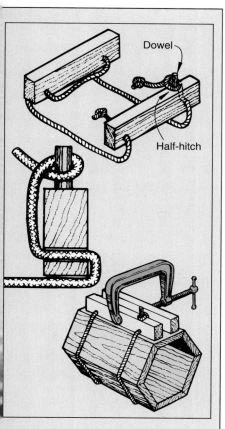

Dowel

Half-hitch

to make a half hitch around the dowel. Then, draw the wooden pieces together with a C-clamp or hand-screw to tighten.

—*Joe Bailey, Russellville, Ark.*

How to get glue into those dowel holes

Applying adhesive to the walls of a dowel hole without making a gluey mess of the area around the rim of the hole can be difficult

TIP: Apply the glue with a bent-over pipe cleaner as shown at right. You can get the correct amount of glue onto the necessary surfaces without a mess, then discard the inexpensive pipe cleaner.

—*Ralph A. Sprang, Jr, Columbia, Md.*

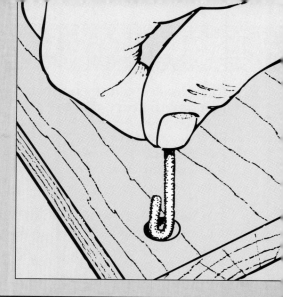

Plastic electrical tape holds glue joints together

Tape sure would be an easy way to clamp glued joints on a small box. Too bad masking tape tears when you try to stretch it around sharp edges.

TIP: Short-circuit that torn-tape problem with black plastic electrical tape. It resists tearing, even on sharp corners, and its stretchiness lets you pull joints up snug.

—*Charles Von Herrmann, Columbia, S.C.*

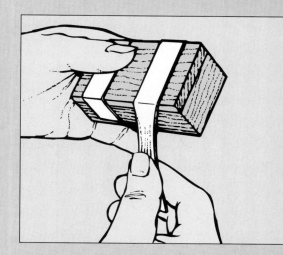

Shop vacuum gets glue where it's needed

Trying to force glue into a tight spot such as a crack on a board or a split in an old furniture part can exasperate even the most patient woodworker. And sometimes the spot that needs the glue is so tight you can't even get a hypodermic needle in there.

TIP: Place the board so the place you need to glue hangs over the end of your bench. Now, bring over your shop vacuum, turn it on, and hold the nozzle underneath. Apply glue to the top, letting the suction pull it in. When glue comes out the bottom, clamp the workpiece.

—*James Reister, Walla Walla, Wash.*

Fastening and Gluing

Base makes miter clamps handier to store and use

Your vise-type miter clamps take up a lot of drawer space between uses. It would be handier to hang them up, but they don't lend themselves to that.

TIP: Make a ¾" scrapwood base with a hanging hole for each clamp. Set the clamp on your stock, and trace around it. Leave extra material for the base at the back of the clamp where shown *below*. Bandsaw or scrollsaw along the base outline, and drill a 1" (or other convenient size) hanging hole where shown. Attach the clamp to the base. In addition to providing a handy hanging hole, the base elevates the clamp above the bench, making the handles easier to turn.

—*David Hoague, Warren, R.I.*

A cam-do carving hold-down

For safe and effective carving of flat work-pieces, you must secure the carving in a way that frees both of your hands and doesn't mar your masterpiece. It sure would be nice to have a hold-down that adapts to any carving.

TIP: Drill a series of ½" holes, set apart 2" on center, into a piece of ¾×12×18" plywood (or larger if desired). Then, make at least two T-shaped pins from 1¼" lengths of ½" dowel and ¾" lengths of 1" dowel such as those shown *above*. Drill a ½" hole, ½" deep, into the center of the 1" dowel lengths and glue and insert the ½" dowel pieces. From ¾" solid stock, cut a cam according to the full-sized pattern *above*, and drill a ½" hole as indicated. Glue a 1¾" length of ½" dowel into the hole in the cam so ½" of dowel protrudes from each face. Now, you can hold a carving of most any shape between at least two pins and the cam. Clamp the board to your workbench or hold it in your lap, whatever's most comfortable to you.

—*Gordon Humphrey, Victoria, B.C.*

Plumbing part grips clamps for easy gluing

Clamping a large glue-up with pipe clamps can turn into a wrestling match. The task becomes much easier if you secure the clamps to a clamping table, but finding a way to attach the clamps to the table can become quite a battle, too.

TIP: Plastic holders for ¾" plastic plumbing pipe, such as the ones shown *below*, provide an inexpensive, effective solution. Steel ¾" pipe snaps right in, and the holder has enough grip to keep the clamp from tipping over while you lay your glued-up stock in place. Mount the holders on two ¾×1" strips, spaced to meet your needs, and then attach the strips to a piece of plywood to make a portable clamping table. Available from hardware stores homecenters, or plumbing shops, the pipe holders ordinarily cost about 15 cents apiece.

—*H. Dick Reynolds, Jr, Mediapolis, Iowa*

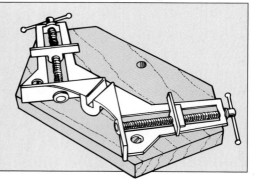

Plastic plumbing pipe holders

¾" pipe clamps

Open the door to convenient clamping

You start to feel awfully clumsy when clamping small woodworking projects, what with trying to hold the clamp, the pieces, and the protective pads while turning the clamp screw.

TIP: This light-duty clamp sits on the bench to take the pressure off you and put it on the work where it belongs. It does the job without clamp screws because it's really a quick-release doorstop.

To build the jig, assemble a frame of ¾-thick scrapwood like the one shown *below.* (Select dimensions to meet your own needs.) Then, mount the doorstop where shown. (Build one with multiple doorstops for larger work.) To clamp, simply push the plunger to press the workpiece against the back of the jig. To release, push the lever toward the doorstop body.

You also could adapt doorstops to secure work on a drill-press table, miter box, or other equipment. Hardware stores and home centers sell the doorstops.

—*Lloyd Prailes, Boulder Junction, Wis.*

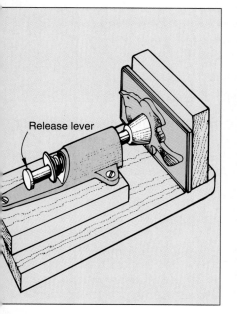

Release lever

Paint bottles promote better biscuit gluing

Gently, you squeeze the bottle of glue, aiming to inject a bit of adhesive into a biscuit slot. And then, splurt! As you wipe up the spilled glue you notice there still isn't as much glue as you wanted in the biscuit slot.

TIP: With soap and water, wash out an empty 2-oz. plastic bottle for acrylic paint, the kind tole painters use. Pour some glue into the container and screw on the top. The small opening, about ⅛" or so, lets you squeeze out small amounts of glue precisely where you want them, even into slots for small no. 0 biscuits. The bottle's flip-top lid seals tightly.

—*Sheila Heckman, Shartlesville, Pa.*

GLUE

Size 0 biscuit

Keep mitered corners aligned while gluing

Misalignment can botch any mitered corner. It's impossible to hide poor joinery here, so make sure you get it right.

TIP: Cut several 4×4" blocks from a plastic-laminate countertop. Clamp these blocks with the laminate toward the workpiece. The plastic resists the glue and the blocks will hold the pieces in flush alignment.

—*Richard Hopkins, St. Louis*

Microwave dowels for a better fit

Moisture in the air can swell dowel pins so they don't fit. Forcing them runs the risk of splitting the bored pieces.

TIP: Shrink those dowels by placing them on a paper towel or plate inside a microwave oven set on "HIGH" for 30 seconds. Remove, and check the pins for fit. Microwave them for an additional 15 or 30 seconds if necessary.

—*from the* **WOOD** *magazine shop*

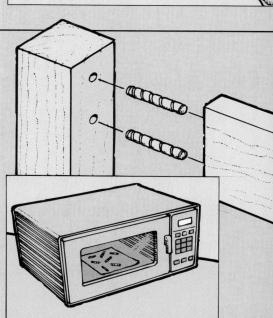

Fastening and Gluing

Jig holds panels on edge

Clamping any long narrow object on edge requires a door buck or other specialized equipment that most home woodworkers don't own.

TIP: Clamp large, objects vertically with these two right-angle jigs. Glue and screw together these jigs from ¾" plywood. Place threaded inserts in your workbench at regular intervals, and fasten each jig to the workbench with a thumbscrew and washer. Secure your workpiece to the front of the jigs with C-clamps, and you're ready to work.

—*Bob Shermer, Los Osos, Calif.*

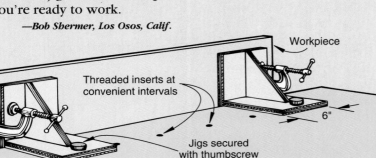

¾"
¾" plywood stock
Thumbscrew
Washer
7½"
¾"
Workbench top
8¾"
Threaded insert

Workpiece
Threaded inserts at convenient intervals
6"
Jigs secured with thumbscrew

Wooden clamp corners clamp corners better

Metal corner brackets supplied with some strap-type woodworking clamps can hinder rather than help a woodworker. Rounded corners crush the wood, and the sharp edges can quickly mar fine wood.

TIP: Improve the strap clamp with wooden corners. Crosscut a 90° V-groove about ⅜" deep ¾" from one end of a 12"–long hardwood 1×6" or 1×8". Do this by tilting your saw blade to 45° and making a pass from each edge. Cut a ⅛" kerf ⅛" deep in the center of the groove. Cut off the machined end, centering the groove on the piece. Rout a ¼" or ⅜" round-over on the back edges.

Cut four equal corner blocks, and sand. The kerfed V-groove prevents corner damage—and gluing the block to your project.

—*Brian Schaible, San Diego, Calif.*

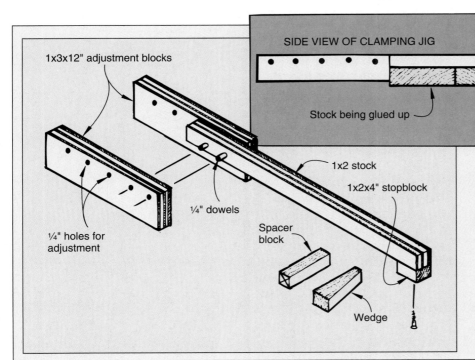

1x3x12" adjustment blocks
¼" dowels
¼" holes for adjustment
Spacer block
Wedge
1x2 stock
1x2x4" stopblock

SIDE VIEW OF CLAMPING JIG
Stock being glued up
Spacer block
Wedge

Scrapwood eases pressure caused by clamp shortage

After you gather all of your clamps together, you're one short of the number you'd like to have for an edge-gluing job.

TIP: Build a clamp from scrapwood. Select a piece of 1×2" stock about 18" longer than the width of your assembled stock. Attach a 1×2×4" stop block at one end, and

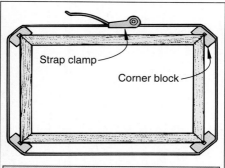

Strap clamp

Corner block

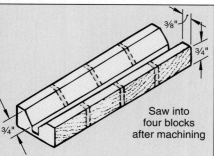

3/8"

3/4"

3/4"

Saw into four blocks after machining

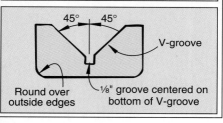

45°   45°

V-groove

Round over outside edges

1/8" groove centered on bottom of V-groove

then drill two dowel holes 2" apart in the other end as shown. Insert dowels so that they extend 1" from each side of the clamp board. Then, drill dowel holes on 2" centers through two 1×3×12" pieces for the adjustment blocks.

To use, place the clamp board over the work to be glued. Slip an adjustment block over the dowels on each side, placing them to allow about an inch of extra width between the work and the clamp slot. Then, place a spacer block and a wooden wedge at the fixed end of the clamp slot and drive the wedge into clamp the work.

—*Dan Cranery, Oak Ridge, N.J.*

A sticky solution for a screwy problem

Sometimes, tight quarters restrict you from steadying a screw with one hand while you turn a screwdriver with your other hand.

TIP: Drop a small dab of hot-melt glue onto the head of the fastener, and attach the screwdriver or ratchet with the glue. When you finish driving the fastener, the tool will release easily. A little scraping removes any residual adhesive.

—*David J. Casolino, Milford, Conn.*

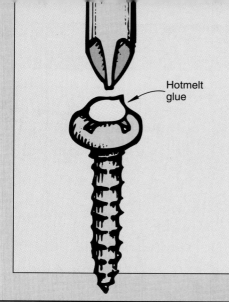

Hotmelt glue

How to make your clamps project-friendly

To protect your projects from metal clamp pads, you have to add small scrap blocks. But, it takes time to find the right block and then position it.

TIP: Solve these difficulties by making clamping blocks for the swivel end of your clamps as shown in the drawing at *right*. Bore holes for the swivel pad. Drill pilot holes and add wood screws where needed.

—*Walter Roberts, Tempe, Ariz.*

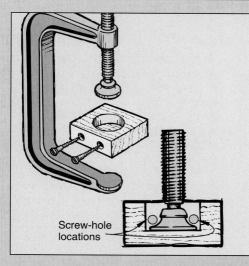

Screw-hole locations

A modified carriage bolt with lots of grip

Carriage bolts deserve a place in any fastener arsenal, but the heads of these handy items lose their gripping power after you remove and replace them several times. The problem: The hole becomes too worn to hold the bolt:

TIP: Give the bolt a no-slip profile by cutting or grinding away opposite sides of the head as shown at *right*. Then, with a straight bit of appropriate size, rout a groove to hold the modified bolt head. Set the bit depth to match the height of the bolt head.

—*Joseph Mock, Columbus, Ohio*

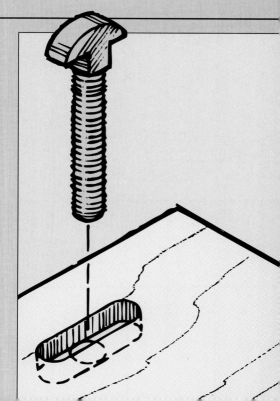

Finishing

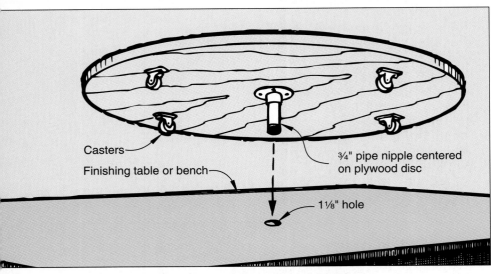

Casters

Finishing table or bench

¾" pipe nipple centered on plywood disc

1⅛" hole

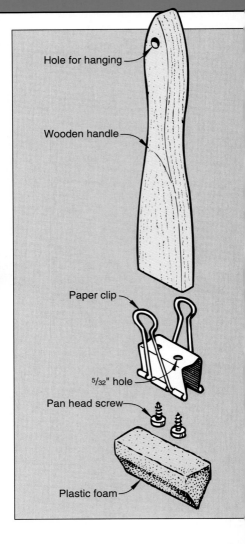

Hole for hanging

Wooden handle

Paper clip

⁵/₃₂" hole

Pan head screw

Plastic foam

Turntable makes it easy to spray finishes

Spraying finish or paint can be tricky for beginners and old hands alike, particularly if you have too little space to move readily around the project as you wield the spray-gun or spray can.

TIP: Build a turntable to use on top of your workbench or finishing table. First, from ¾" plywood, cut a piece with a 3' diameter and screw a ¾" pipe flange at its cen-ter. Near the perimeter, attach four or more swivel plate casters, as shown in the illustration *above*. Finally, thread a pipe nipple into the flange and drill a hole in the top of your bench to receive the nipple that serves as a turntable pivot. Placing projects on this handy device allows you to rotate them easily after you finish spraying each side.

—Kenneth Boyd, Tablequah, Okla.

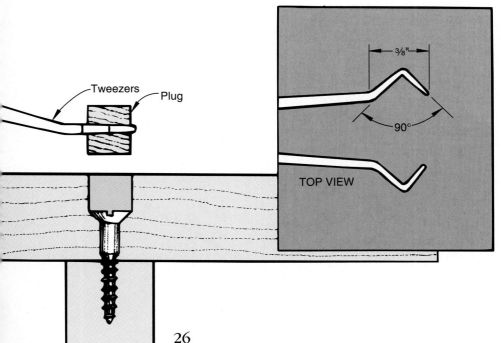

Tweezers   Plug

3⁄8"

90°

TOP VIEW

Altered tweezers grab those pesky plugs

Inserting a plug over a counter-sunk screw head often becomes a vexing, messy task. Trying to hang on to the glue-coated plug while lining it up and tapping it into place can make even the most skilled woodworker feel like a fumble-fingered incompetent.

TIP: Stop by the drugstore and buy a pair of tweezers, large ones with angled tips. Heat the ends with a propane torch and re-form them, as shown at *left*, with needle-nosed pliers. With the modified tweezers, you'll have a firm grip on the plugs and your fingers won't be getting in the way.

—Robert Shermer, Loss Osos, Calif.

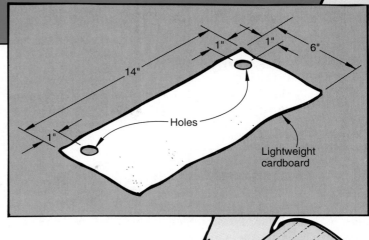

Homemade brush features renewable foam "bristles"

For a small finishing job, there's nothing like a disposable foam brush for convenience. But just when you need one, you often find you've disposed of them all.

TIP: You'll always have a clean brush on hand for small jobs if you take a few minutes now to make a renewable foam brush. Bandsaw or scrollsaw the handle from a piece of scrapwood about ¾×1¼×7". Then, drill two ⁵⁄₃₂" holes in a spring paper clip where shown, and attach the clip to the handle with two #6×½" panhead sheet metal screws. (The medium-sized clip shown measures ⅝" wide, and has 1¼"-long jaws.)

For the applicator, cut a piece of ½"-thick plastic foam to 1×1¼". (Bevel the end, if you like.) To use, grip the foam in the paper clip. Afterwards, just throw the foam away and insert a new piece so you'll be ready next time.

—Bob Dahlberg, Boulder, Colo.

Cardboard sanitizes messy paint pouring

Pouring paint or other finishing materials from a can practically guarantees a mess.

TIP: Reduce the dribbles and drips with a simple paint-can spout. Just cut a pair of ¾"-diameter finger holes where shown on a 6×14" piece of cardboard. Then bend the cardboard into an arc and slip it into the lid groove around the top of the can. Hold the spout in place with a finger through each hole, as shown at *right*, as you pour.

—Darin Botts, Bloomington, Minn.

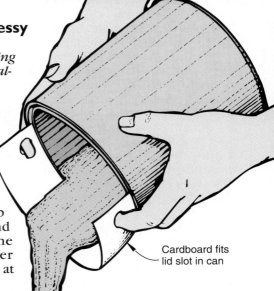

Cardboard fits lid slot in can

Smooth on the filler with a shop-made tool

Sometimes you have to use wood filler, but putting it on with a putty knife leaves something to be desired. Putty knives always seem to be the wrong size, or the metal blade scars your wood.

TIP: Make an applicator from scraps of hardwood from 1" to 1¼" thick. Cut a wedge-shaped piece as shown in the side view at *left*, and sand the thin end to width with a drum sander. Apply filler with the long, tapered end of the applicator, and remove the excess with the opposite end. If you don't get the filler cleaned off your applicator before it sets up, just sand down to a new surface.

—Stan Thomas, Bend, Ore.

TOP VIEW

1-1¼"

6½"

SIDE VIEW

1¼"

Finishing

Fixture holds frames for easy finishing

When it comes time for finishing a picture frame, you often end up pushing it all over the benchtop. Most are just too light to stay put while you brush on finish, especially on the edges.

TIP: Build this fixture from a piece of plywood and four dowels, and you'll fear frame finishing no more. On the ¾" plywood base, draw a rectangle the same size as the inside of the rabbeted opening in the frame (5×7" for a frame that holds a 5×7" photo, for example). Drill a ¼" hole inside the pencil line at each corner, angling it outward about 3°. Insert a 4" length of ¼" dowel into each hole. For finishing a frame, press it onto the dowels—the tension created by forcing the dowels toward vertical will hold the frame firmly. You'll be able to reach the edges easily, too.

—Gene Washer, Shelburne Falls, Mass.

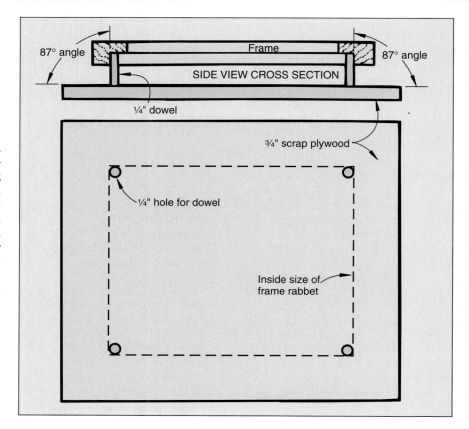

87° angle

Frame

87° angle

SIDE VIEW CROSS SECTION

¼" dowel

¾" scrap plywood

¼" hole for dowel

Inside size of frame rabbet

When project painting, not finger painting, is the object

Painting a small part, especially a ball, often results in a better coat of paint on your fingers than on the thing you're trying to paint. Then, you have to figure out some way to set it down to dry.

TIP: Screw tongue depressors to a scrapwood block. Drill a hole through the other end of each tongue depressor, and drive a screw into each one. Clamp the object between the screw points for painting (and set the whole thing aside for drying). Stretch a rubber band around the tongue depressors for more tension.

—Jim Mayer, Lake Lotawana, Mo.

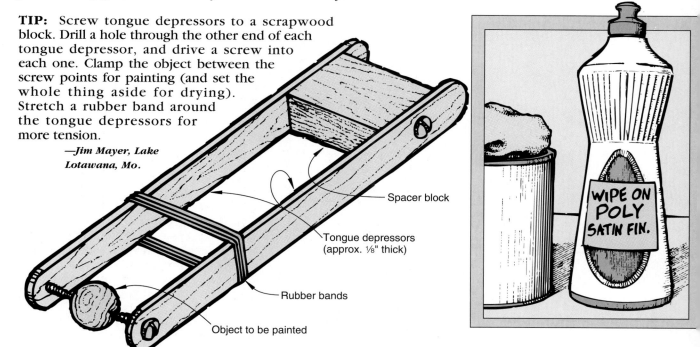

Spacer block

Tongue depressors (approx. ⅛" thick)

Rubber bands

Object to be painted

WIPE ON POLY SATIN FIN.

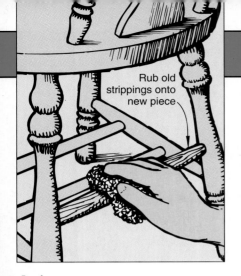

Rub old strippings onto new piece

Aging new parts for old furniture

Buying old furniture in need of serious repairs can be a bargain for the person willing to fix it up and refinish it. One major hurdle: making new parts match the color of the original parts.

TIP: Disassemble the piece of furniture to be restored and use wood that matches in species and grain to construct any replacement parts. Reassemble the parts before stripping the varnish or other finish on them. Now, cover the replacement parts with dirty strippings and wipe off. About the third time you do this, you won't be able to distinguish the new part from the old ones.

—*Bill Perkins, Roachdale, Ind.*

Dish detergent bottle puts the squeeze on messy finish

Wipe-on urethane products offer convenience and great looks, but dipping the wiping rag into the can makes a mess.

TIP: After you've squeezed the last of the liquid dish detergent out of its plastic bottle, clean the bottle, and fill it with the wipe-on finish. Now, at finishing time, simply pull the spout open and squeeze the right amount onto your rag. Push the spout closed for storage. Be sure to label the bottle.

—*Soterios Lallas, Viroqua, Wis.*

A steamy solution for wood indentations

Small dents often crop up on the surfaces of workpieces before you complete a project. You could fill the indentations with putty, but these repairs rarely blend in naturally. Applying a wet cloth to the dent and heating it with an iron sometimes raises the wood fibers, but not always.

TIP: With a hand-held clothing steamer or iron, shoot some steam onto the affected area. The steam will raise the wood fibers of shallow indentations, allowing you to re-level the area with a little light sanding.

—*Kerry Kumlien, Milton, Wis.*

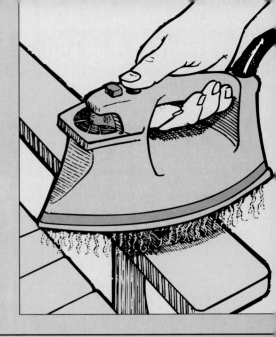

Brush wiper cuts paint mess

Every time you wipe your brush on the edge of a paint can, you get a little more paint into the groove. Pretty soon, you have paint dripping down the side.

TIP: Stretch a piece of reinforced strapping tape across the top of the opened can and pinch the sticky sides together to make a terrific brush-wiping edge. Duct tape or masking tape would work just as well, too.

—*Herbert Akers, Rockville, Md.*

Strapping tape

Tape bristles together for a substitute stencil brush

When you have a small amount of stenciling to do, it's tempting to avoid the expense of buying a stencil brush by daubing the paint on with a standard brush. Trouble is, an ordinary brush isn't stiff enough for stenciling. Then, too, you could end up ruining a good brush that way.

TIP: Before you try to stencil with your standard paintbrush, wrap masking tape around the bristles. The tightly bundled bristles will be stiff enough for stenciling. The tape will also keep the bristles from splaying out and breaking off. After the job, simply remove the tape. Your brush will be unharmed.

—*Barbara Maxwell, Cuyahoga Falls, Ohio*

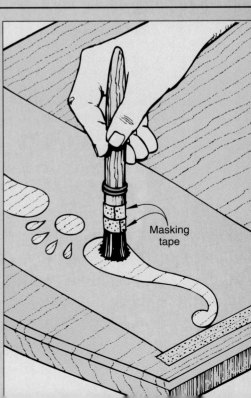

Masking tape

Finishing

Set paint on a paddle for a clean benchtop

Finish cans leave drips and rings that mar your benchtop. Even if you put down papers, some of the finish may soak through and make a mess, anyway.

TIP: Just cut a rectangular paddle similar to the one shown to fit the finish-can size you're using. Add three ¾×¾" strips, placing the two side ones on a slight angle to create a wedge-shaped opening to hold the can securely. Drill a hole in the end of the handle so you can hang the paddle up between uses.

—Jack Brown, Noank, Conn.

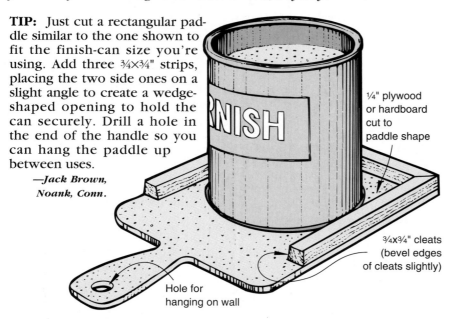

¼" plywood or hardboard cut to paddle shape

¾x¾" cleats (bevel edges of cleats slightly)

Hole for hanging on wall

Patches of putty show true colors

The wood filler you put into a bunch of nail holes didn't match the wood at all. And then it stained so dark that your project has little dots on it now. The unfilled nail holes looked better.

TIP: Make a color chart for wood fillers and putty. On uni-

Tiny plugs make nail holes nearly invisible

You can buy all kinds of fillers for disguising the holes that remain after countersinking finishing nails, but these often leave telltale results.

TIP: From a piece of scrap that matches your work stock, use leather hole punches to cut tiny plugs to match the size of the nail holes. Set the nails slightly below the surface, and dab a little glue into the indentation

with a wood sliver or a paper clip. Then, press the plug into place, making sure the grain of the plug matches the workpiece. It takes a sharp eye to spot these plugs.

—Bill Blain, Edmonton, Alberta

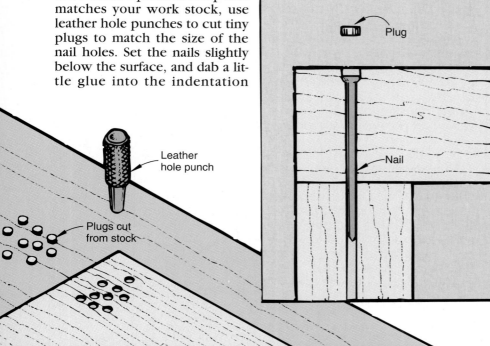

Leather hole punch

Plugs cut from stock

Plug

Nail

Plastic jug helps keep air and sprayer clean

When cleaning a sprayer, you can end up filling the air with paint and thinner. This is environmentally shaky and wasteful to boot.

TIP: Rinse a one-gallon plastic bleach bottle thoroughly and cut a 4×4" hole in the side. Then, glue a woven dishwashing scrubber over the hole with silicone adhesive. Heavy cloth such as canvas or denim would work also. Now, clean the gun by spraying into the top of the jug. The thinner will stay inside the jug. If vapor does escape through the jug openings, reduce your sprayer pressure. After the thinner sits for a while, the impurities will settle out and you can reuse the clean thinner.

—Tom Haltmeyer, Peoria, Ariz.

form-sized samples of woods you commonly use, drill ½" holes about ¼" deep. Fill each hole with a different putty or filler, let it set, and sand. Apply your usual stains and finishes to some of the samples, then label each one. Now, when you need to pick a filler, just compare the wood you're using to the test patches to find a good match.

—Charles Howard,
Middleburg, Va.

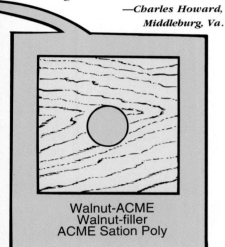

Walnut-ACME
Walnut-filler
ACME Sation Poly

Solution for small-part finishing

Painting, staining, and finishing small pieces frustrates most woodworkers because the objects refuse to stay put as you brush or spray them. Using your fingers to hold the pieces can be messy, and the finish may adhere the objects to your work surface.

TIP: Build a finishing box such as the one shown *above*. From ¾" stock, cut the sides, top, and bottom of a 4×10×20" box (or larger if necessary). Clamp the top and bottom pieces together and drill ¼" through holes simultaneously to ensure alignment. Unclamp the assembly, and epoxy 3" lengths of ¼" steel rod with sharpened points into the bottom holes. Enlarge the top holes just slightly to permit free, but not sloppy, up-and-down movement of 8"-long sharpened rods. With the box assembled, you can coat small pieces of most any shape without fear of making fingerprints and smudges.

—W. P. Locke, Huntington Beach, Calif.

For a satin finish, apply gloss first

Satin or semigloss varnishes contain dulling agents that can cloud your finish after the necessary multiple applications.

TIP: When you want a satin finish, apply the same brand of gloss varnish for the undercoats. The gloss finish doesn't cloud up as much, and its reflective surface reveals flaws better. And, you can easily tell which areas have received less sanding than others. Finally, add a satin top coat.

—Kenneth R. Thornley
West Hartford, Conn.

Extra countersink ensures a tight joint

After tightening the screws joining two project parts, you notice a small gap between the pieces. Tightening the screws doesn't help close the gap.

TIP: Here's what happened: The screw thread pulled the wood fibers, raising a bump around the screw hole. That bump prevents the pieces from fitting closely. Here's what to do about it: After drilling the pilot hole and shank hole, countersink each slightly on the mating surface. Then, assemble the parts with a gap-free joint.

—*Tom Xedos, Moreno Valley, Calif.*

Bump

Countersink shank and pilot holes slightly

Staples make sure corners stay square

Miter-cut corners make gluing tough. You get the corners square dry-clamping them, but then they go haywire when you try to assemble them again with glue.

TIP: Square the corners in a strap-type clamp. With everything just right, turn the assembly over and staple each corner. Remove the clamp and spread each joint enough to inject glue into it from the top with a syringe-type applicator. Then, reclamp the frame, which is still square, thanks to the staples. After the glue sets, remove the staples.

—*Max Sageser, Earth, Texas*

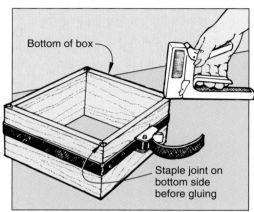
Bottom of box
Staple joint on bottom side before gluing

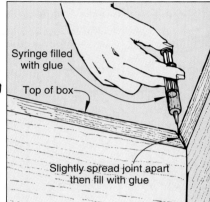
Syringe filled with glue
Top of box
Slightly spread joint apart then fill with glue

Some spadework makes a trying job easier

You're having a terrible time driving threaded brass inserts into ½" holes in your project. You can't guide them in straight because the screwdriver slips out of the slot, battering the insert and the wood.

TIP: Put the screwdriver aside, and chuck a ½" spade bit into your variable-speed portable drill. The cutting edge of the bit fits into the slot on the insert, and the center pilot prevents the bit from slipping out sideways. Drive the insert at a slow speed. If you use a drill press, turn the chuck by hand to drive the inserts. For other inserts, select a spade bit that matches the pilot-hole diameter.

—*Thomas Kelly, Trenton, N.J.*

Make gauges for quickly setting your plate jointer

On many plate jointers, setting the fence height for various thicknesses of stock can be time-consuming work. It sure would be nice if you could quickly set the fence at predetermined heights. Another tricky task: keeping the fence parallel to the workpiece.

TIP: Solve both problems by making a set of gauges from scrap. To start, place your plate jointer on a flat table so its base rests flush with the surface. Use a piece of material of the desired thickness and set the fence for a centered cut. For 1½"-and-thicker stock, it makes sense to center two slots. Mark the blocks for material thickness and number of biscuits.

To set the fence, place the jointer on a table, loosen and lift the fence, place the correct block under it, and tighten the fence locking screws while holding it against the block.

—*Bob Hockenberry, Rochester, Minn.*

Center saw kerf on several different thicknesses of blocks to keep as guides
Plate jointer
¾"
Scrap block

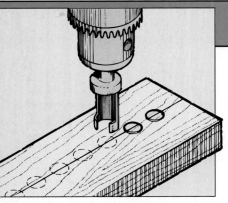

Surefire plug alignment

To hide wooden plugs, it helps to align the grain of the plugs with the grain of the workpiece. However, sometimes—particularly on small plugs—you can't tell which way the grain runs.

TIP: Before cutting the plugs, draw a pencil mark parallel to the grain as shown *above*. The mark guides you when gluing the plugs in place, and disappears when you sand the plugs flush.

—Richard Rentfrow, Raleigh, N.C.

Here's a plug for end-grain joinery

You hate to drive screws into end grain because they can pull right out. But sometimes, you can't avoid driving them into the end of a board, such as in the case of the bed hardware shown at right.

TIP: For a strong joint, give the screw some face grain to dig into. Here's how: Drill a dowel-diameter hole through the face of the project part, located so that the screw threads will fall mostly or completely inside the hole. Then, glue a length of dowel into the hole. Set the grain on the end of the dowel perpendicular to the grain on the face of the project part. Cut the ends flush with your project part. Now, drill your pilot holes and drive in the screws.

—Tom E. Moore, Madison, Va.

Pull the plug on tenoning troubles

You could turn a round tenon on square stock. But, what if you don't have a lathe?

TIP: Make those round tenons with a tablesaw, drill press, and plug cutter. After determining the tenon dimensions (for example, a ¾" diameter, ⅝"-long tenon on 1½"-square stock), subtract the diameter from the thickness of the stock. Set your tablesaw's cutting depth to half that distance (that's ⅜" in our example).

Now, using your tablesaw miter gauge and a stopblock, cut a kerf ⅝" (or your tenon length) from the end of the stock on each face. Be sure to measure from the end of the stock to the farthest side of the blade. (Step 1 *below*.)

Next, chuck a plug cutter the diameter of your tenon into your drill press. Then, holding the workpiece firmly with clamps, center the plug cutter on the end of the stock, start the drill press, and cut the tenon (Step 2.)

—Chuck Hedlund, Des Moines, Iowa

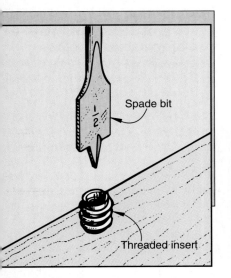

Spade bit

½

Threaded insert

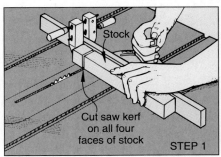

Stock

Cut saw kerf on all four faces of stock

STEP 1

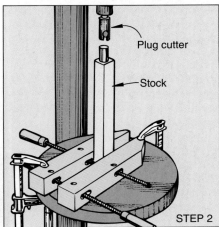

Plug cutter

Stock

STEP 2

Sandpaper secured to template with spray adhesive

Underside of template for dovetail jig

Fine sandpaper cures troublesome shifting

Many dovetail jigs (and other types of fixtures) rely on plastic or metal guides that clamp to your workpiece. Despite your best efforts to tighten the clamps, that slick guide may not stay precisely in place on the smooth wood surface, especially when you're pushing a tool against it.

TIP: Cut a piece of fine sandpaper (maybe 220 or 320 grit) to fit the side of the fixture that contacts the workpiece. Apply adhesive, such as 3M's 77 Spray Adhesive, on the back of the sandpaper, and attach it to the fixture. The sandpaper provides friction, reducing the chance that your fixture guide will creep out of position.

—Ty Powe, San Dimas, Calif.

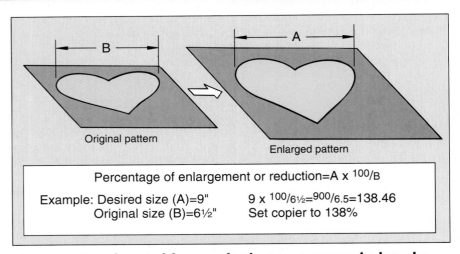

Percentage of enlargement or reduction=A x $^{100}/_B$

Example: Desired size (A)=9"
Original size (B)=6½"

9 x $^{100}/_{6½}$=$^{900}/_{6.5}$=138.46
Set copier to 138%

As your teacher told you, algebra can come in handy

You've stacked up a bunch of photocopies at a dime each, trying to hit the right percentage for enlarging or reducing a pattern. Isn't there some way to figure this out ahead of time?

TIP: Remember high school algebra? Use it now to determine the enlargement or reduction ratio you need. Simply multiply the size you want the pattern to be (A) by 100. Then, divide that number by the original pattern size (B) to find your percentage. Of course, both numbers must be in the same unit of measurement, such as inches or millimeters.

For example: Say you want to enlarge the 6½"-wide heart shown below to 9" wide. A, the size you want, is 9". B, the size you have is 6½". A times 100 equals 900. Enter that on your calculator. Punch the division button, and then enter value B, (6.5). Hit the equals button, and read your answer: 138.46. Enlarge your original at 138 percent.

It works for reducing a pattern, too. To make a 5" heart from the same pattern, simply divide 500 (the size you want times 100) by 6.5 (the size you have). Round off the answer, 76.92, and set the copier at 77 percent.

—*Reuel Smith, Halifax, Nova Scotia*

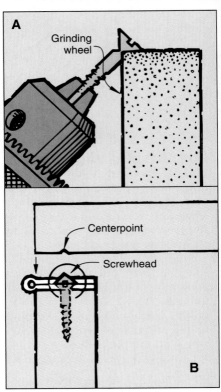

Get right to the point for hinge-screw holes

Even after careful measuring, you can drill pilot holes for hinge screws that leave hinges and doors slightly out of kilter. Then, both the appearance of the project and the smooth swinging of the door suffer from misalignment.

TIP: From flathead wood screws, make concentric-pointed markers for positioning pilot holes on target. First, tighten a screw into the chuck of your portable electric drill. With a grinding wheel and the drill operating simultaneously, remove the head of the screw as shown in Drawing A, *above*. Touch up the newly ground point on the screwhead with a file. After mounting the hinge(s) on the cabinet frame, insert two of these "center finders" into the other half of the hinge, place the door in its correct position as shown in Drawing B, and press it against the hinge to mark the points for drilling pilot holes.

—*Gary Paine, Davison, Mich.*

A starting block sets shelf standards straight

Stray the least bit off the mark when installing shelf standards, and your shelves rock maddeningly. How can you set them straight and steady?

TIP: Fit a spacer block between the cabinet bottom and a slot near the bottom of the shelf standard. Install a shelf clip upside down in the slot, and then rest it on top of the block to position the standard while you drive in the screws or nails. Repeat for the other standards for accurate placement.

—*Lance Lewis, West Newbury, Mass.*

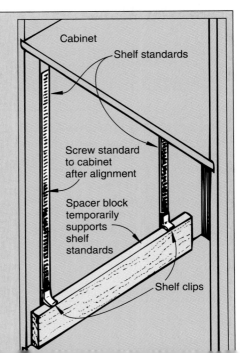

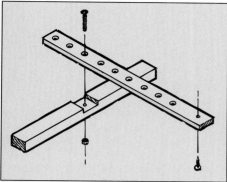

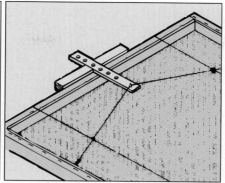

Picture-hanging jig eliminates guesswork

Hanging a picture can be a hit-and-miss affair when you hold the artwork up to a wall and then guess where to position the hanger or nail.

TIP: Make the simple cross-shaped jig, shown in the drawing *above*, by drilling several ¼" holes about 1" apart in a 1×12" piece of ¼" plywood. Then, cut a ¼"-deep, 1"-wide mortise in the center of a 1×10" scrap of ¾" hardwood. Next, add a ¾" self-tapping screw about ½" from one end of the ¼"-thick piece.

Now, lay down the ¾"-thick piece mortise-side-up, and place the ¼"-thick piece into the mortise so the screw points up. Fasten together the two pieces with a ¼" nut and 1¼"-long ¼" bolt. Place the bolt in any hole that suits the size of your picture as shown *above*. With the picture wire draped over the exposed screw point, position the picture on your wall and give the jig a light tap when you find the right spot. The resulting mark from the screw point will tell you exactly where to place the hanger.

—From the WOOD magazine shop

Proportional scale makes changing dimensions easy

Changing the size of a project leads to cumbersome math at times, especially when you want to maintain proportion. For example, you're enlarging a piece that's ⅜" wide and 6" long to 8" long. How wide should it be?

TIP: A graphic artist's proportional scale makes such calculations simple. You just set the original dimension on the rotating circular scale next to the new measurement. Then, each new dimension will be shown right next to the corresponding original. You can set the wheel to a known percentage of enlargement or reduction, too, to determine new measurements. And, it shows you the answers in fractions of an inch, not decimals. (Ours covers a range from ¼" to 90".) You can buy one at an art-supply store for less than $5. By the way, you need to make that piece in our example ½" wide.

—Bill Kuhlmann,
Colorado Springs, Colo.

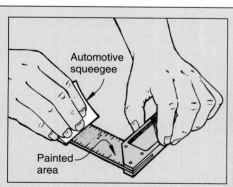

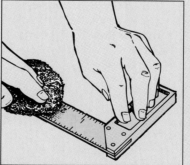

A no-squint improvement for your squares

Most combination and try squares are difficult to read. Why? Their blades have stamped markings that don't contrast sufficiently with the rest of the blade.

TIP: Spray or spread a thin coat of black epoxy enamel paint onto the blade, and then wipe away the excess paint

with a squeegee (the type used for auto-body work) or an old credit card as shown *above left*. This will leave most of the paint in the indentations, making them more visible. After the paint dries, remove any streaks between the indentations with fine-grade steel wool as shown *above right*.

—Raj Chaudbry, Astoria, N.Y.

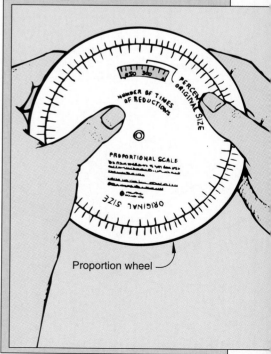

Proportion wheel

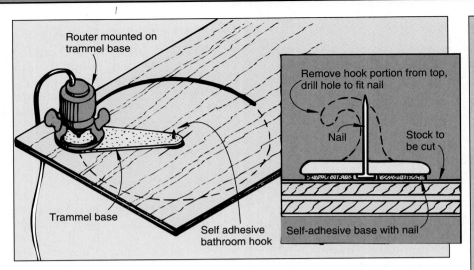

Router mounted on trammel base

Trammel base

Self adhesive bathroom hook

Remove hook portion from top, drill hole to fit nail

Nail

Stock to be cut

Self-adhesive base with nail

This stick-on center solves a sticky cutting problem

Cutting a circular piece with a trammel-mounted router or portable sabersaw leaves a hole right in the middle. What can you do to make a circle without a hole in the middle?

TIP: Make a no-hole centerpoint by modifying a self-adhesive plastic towel hook. (You can buy them in packages at hardware or variety stores.) Cut off the hook and sand the front of the adhesive-backed base flat. At the center,

drill a hole to fit a common nail. Push the nail through from the adhesive side, and cut it off so it protrudes about 1" Trim the adhesive backing around the nail-head and epoxy the nail into position, if necessary.

To use, mark the center of your cutting piece with a large X. Stick the centerpoint over the mark, and put the hole in the trammel arm over the nail. Afterwards, peel the centerpoint off.

—*Bill Lapham, Morgan Hill, Calif.*

Divide disc equally with nut and bolt

You're trying to lay out equally spaced holes around a wheel without a dividing head or protractor. The task is becoming a challenge.

TIP: If you need three or six divisions, you're in luck. Grab a hexheaded bolt that fits through the axle hole, insert the threaded end, and secure the bolt with a nut. Now, extend a line from each hex point to the edge of the wheel. For three divisions, just mark at alternate points.

—*Howard Gaston, Naples, Fla.*

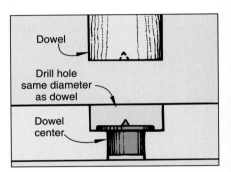

Dowel

Drill hole same diameter as dowel

Dowel center

Dowel center makes quick center finder

Finding and marking the center on a number of same-sized dowels—for a batch of small ornaments, for instance—sure gets tedious. It would be great to find a quicker way to do it.

TIP: Chuck a spade bit the size of the dowel into your drill press, and bore a hole about halfway through a block of hardwood. Next, change to a bit the diameter of a steel dowel center. Piloting on the centerpoint hole left by the spade bit, drill the rest of the way through the block to accept the dowel center. Then, with the center in place, put one end of your dowel into the larger hole, and tap the other end with a mallet. Bingo! An instant center mark.

—*Ray Matthews, Port Clinton, Ohio*

Centering head takes lines around corners

Transferring layout lines from the face of a board to an edge often causes trouble, particularly with a rounded or chamfered edge.

TIP: Slide the rule out and put your combination square's centering head on the job. Align it with the layout mark and square it to the board. Now, mark the new line. For greatest accuracy, make your marks with an awl, X-acto knife, or sharp scriber.

—*Dave Gorman, Corunna, Ontario*

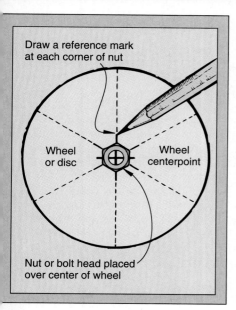

Draw a reference mark
at each corner of nut

Wheel
or disc

Wheel
centerpoint

Nut or bolt head placed
over center of wheel

Modified dowels aid dry-assembly

*When dry-assembling a project
with doweled joints, the dowels
can seize in the holes, making
disassembly difficult.*

TIP: Test-fit parts with dowels
that won't stick in the holes.
Make them by sawing a bandsaw
kerf about half the length of the
dowel from one end. Then, from
the other end, cut another kerf
90° to the first one. The modified
dowels fit snugly enough to align
parts accurately, but you can still
remove them easily. Then glue
the project together with
unmodified dowels.

—D. Higginbotham,
Lawrenceville, Ga.

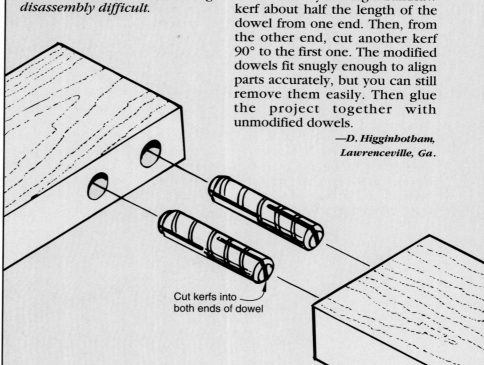

Cut kerfs into
both ends of dowel

File card sets spacing for hooks in tight spots.

*You could go crazy spacing
cup hooks in hard-to-reach
places or where you don't
want layout marks on the finished wood.*

TIP: Cut a notch in a corner
of a file card. Determine the
hook spacing and cut another
notch that distance from the
first one. Then, measure to
the shelf edge and fold the
card as a depth gauge. Now,
slide the card along the shelf
to space your hooks.

—Myron Levy, Gold Hill, Ore.

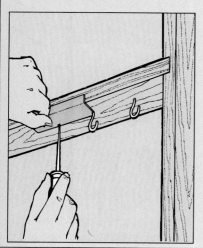

Phillips screwdriver aids assembly in more ways than one

*Everything fits up fine, but now
you need to take your project
apart for finishing, How can you
be sure you'll get the parts back
together just right?*

TIP: Make index marks on mating surfaces and matching parts
with your Phillips screwdriver.
On the back, underside, or some
other inconspicuous spot, put the
screwdriver tip against the wood
and tap the handle to make a
small X. Mark the adjacent piece
the same way. You'll be sure to
see your mark if you make a pair
of X's close together. The screwdriver marks won't disappear
when you sand or finish the project as pencil marks would.

—from the WOOD magazine shop

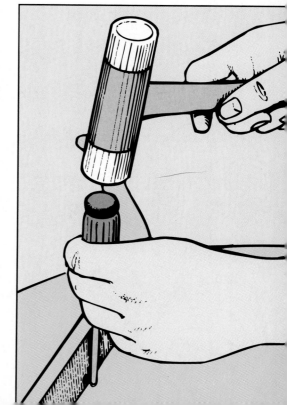

Layout and Measuring

Taped instructions prevent costly goofs

The large cabinet sides you've made from expensive walnut plywood look great. The dadoes and rabbets are straight as a string, and the dimensions are right on the money. Unfortunately, they're both left sides.

TIP: Masking tape can keep you from making the right cuts in the wrong places. Mark the good face, top, or back of the panels with masking-tape labels. Reminders or special instructions on the tape prevent cutting errors and also prove helpful at assembly time.

—*from the* WOOD *magazine shop*

One giant try square

How many times have you worked on a large project and wished you had a try square as big as a carpenter's framing square?

TIP: By adding blocks of wood as shown *above*, you can convert a framing square into an oversized try square for those big jobs. First, cut the blocks to size from ¼"—¾" stock and clamp them in position on the square. Then, drill ⅛" holes completely through the blocks and square blade. Remove the clamps, scuff the blade with 80-grit sandpaper. Then apply epoxy glue to the mating surfaces, and reassemble. Insert ⅛" brass or steel pins of the appropriate length. Hold the assembly together with masking tape until the glue sets, then sand the pins flush with the surfaces of the blocks.

—*Leslie Douette, Prince Edward Island, Canada*

Cut blocks off at a 45° angle

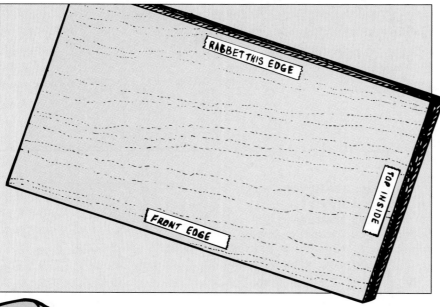

RABBET THIS EDGE

TOP INSIDE

FRONT EDGE

Grind a new angle for an old square

You have some 135° angles to lay out. Fiddling around with the protractor and a straightedge is pretty clumsy work, though.

TIP: Add another angle to an old combination square. Grind the corner of the blade as shown *below*. Now, just set the angled end of the modified blade flush with the 45° side of the head and you'll be ready to measure that obtuse angle.

—*Clay Addison, Charlotte, N.C.*

'Wrenching' solution for misplaced calipers

Suppose you have to determine the diameter of a piece of pipe or dowel, but calipers aren't to be found in your shop. How can you take the measurement?

TIP: Slip an adjustable wrench over the piece, tighten snugly, and then use a tape measure to determine the jaw opening.

—*from the* WOOD *magazine shop*

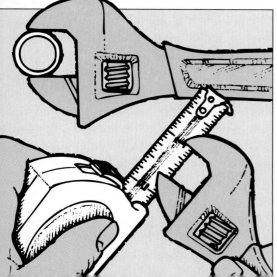

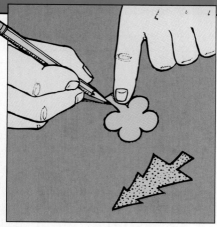

Template with 'true grit'

Tracing around miniature templates made of paper or thin scrapwood can be difficult because the pattern tends to slip.

TIP: After transferring the shape onto the back of 60-grit sandpaper, cut out the shape with heavy scissors or straight-cut tin snips. Place the pattern face down and apply finger pressure to keep it in place as you trace around it.

—*Al Schlabach, Flora, Ill.*

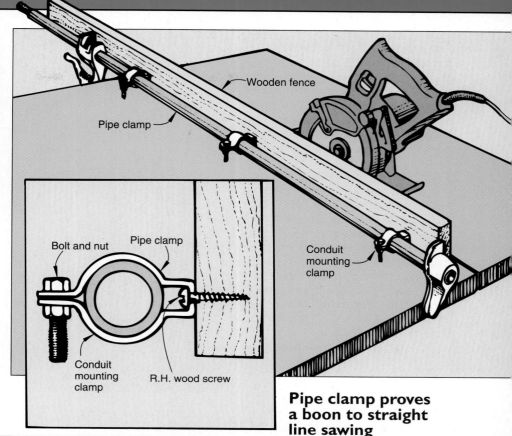

Wooden fence

Pipe clamp

Conduit mounting clamp

Bolt and nut

Pipe clamp

Conduit mounting clamp

R.H. wood screw

Pipe clamp proves a boon to straight line sawing

A portable circular saw often turns out to be the handiest tool you have for crosscutting large sheets of plywood. Without a guide, however, you'll have a tough time making a straight cut.

TIP: With a pipe clamp, a straight piece of 1×4 stock, and a few pieces of hardware, construct an adjustable fence for your circular saw. (It works great with a router, too.) Choose a pipe clamp that spans the sheet you're cutting, and then cut the 1×4 fence to that width. Attach the fence to the clamp with standoff conduit clamps, as shown in the detail drawing *above*, which prevent interference between the fence and the clamp. Close each conduit clamp with a bolt long enough to act as a leg to keep the fence from tipping. Cover the end of the bolt with tape or foam to prevent scratching the material.

—*George Williams, Elk Grove, Calif.*

A mini-bevel made from hacksaw blades does a big-time job

There's nothing like a bevel gauge for transferring and marking angles accurately. When you're working in a tight spot, though, a standard gauge may be too large.

TIP: Make a smaller bevel gauge from the ends of an old hacksaw blade. Break the blade about 2½" from each end. Now, with the untoothed edges facing out, overlap the two pieces and rivet them together through the end holes. Make the joint tight enough that the gauge will hold an angle setting. Grind rounded corners on the broken ends. Grind the rivet as flat as possible, too.

—*D. B. Gonzalez Jr, Pensacola, Fla.*

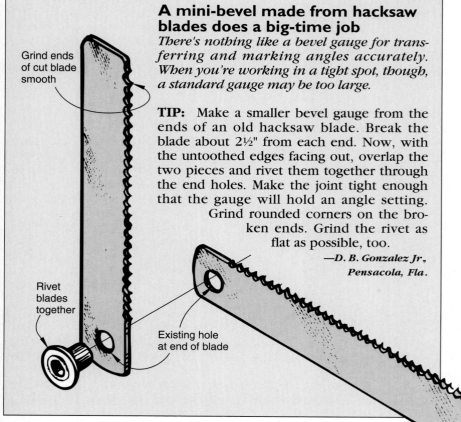

Grind ends of cut blade smooth

Rivet blades together

Existing hole at end of blade

Shop Organizers

Go to a corner to store an abundance of stock

If you have unlimited shop space, stop reading here. For the rest of us, storing project material poses a major problem. Just one full sheet of plywood covers up a big portion of precious wall space.

TIP: Move your materials into a corner. As shown at *right*, you can stow everything from full sheets of plywood (if your shop has 8' or more of headroom) to cut-off pieces into an area that extends only 40" along each wall. Construct the dividers from plywood and 2×2 stock, and attach them to the floor and ceiling. Add shelves to hold cut-off pieces and small stock, if desired

—*Doug Parker, Grandville, Mich.*

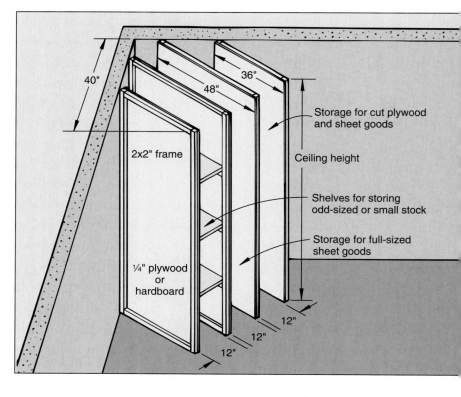

40"

2x2" frame

¼" plywood or hardboard

48"

36"

Storage for cut plywood and sheet goods

Ceiling height

Shelves for storing odd-sized or small stock

Storage for full-sized sheet goods

12"

12"

12"

Storing big sheets easier with rollers

Wrestling sheets of plywood in and out of tight storage spaces is not only tiring, it's also likely to damage the edges of the sheet.

TIP: Improve your plywood storage area by incorporating rollers like those shown *below*. Cut the wheels from ¾" stock with a 2½"

holesaw and put them on wood or metal axles. Now, you can easily slide individual sheets in or out of the storage slot. In this case, we placed a new 2×4 framework about 6" in front of a wall. Perforated hardboard on front holds tools and makes space for sheet material behind.

—*Mick Dirr, Cincinnati, Ohio*

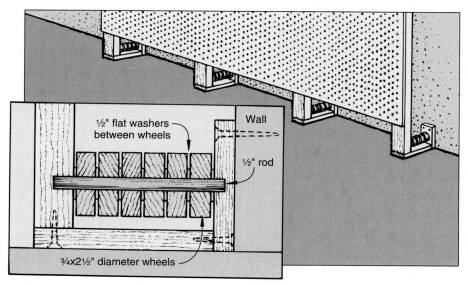

½" flat washers between wheels

Wall

½" rod

¾x2½" diameter wheels

Saws stay straight and sharp in hanging rack

Tossing your handsaws into a drawer or toolbox is an invitation to dull teeth, and maybe a kinked, or warped blade. Yet, hanging them on a toolboard takes a lot of space.

TIP: Here's a saw rack that stores up to five saws in a 10"-wide space. And it makes putting them away properly a snap. Cut the cams, compartment sides, and back from maple or other hardwood using the dimensions shown in the drawing at *right*. Attach the compartment sides to the back with screws and glue, and then secure the cams where shown. Make sure the cams move freely. Hang the holder.

Now, to use, slide the saw in from the bottom, pushing the cam up. When you release the saw, the cam will trap the saw blade against the side.

—*E. Q. Smith, M.D., West Hills, Calif.*

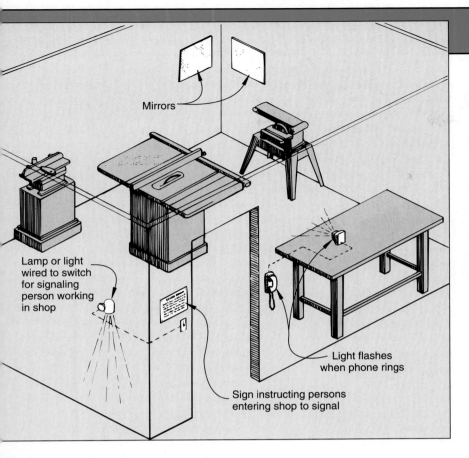

Mirrors

Lamp or light wired to switch for signaling person working in shop

Sign instructing persons entering shop to signal

Light flashes when phone rings

Flashing lights announce phone calls and visitors

Concentrating on your project with your earplugs in, the dust collector turned on, and a power tool running, it's not surprising that you might not hear the telephone ring. The same situation makes it easy for a visitor to enter your workshop without your knowing. A tap on the shoulder or a greeting from an unnoticed guest is guaranteed to cause a shriek, or worse, an accident.

TIP: To avoid missing telephone calls when you're in the shop, install a flashing-light telephone signal. Radio Shack outlets and other sources sell a plug-in device that connects to your telephone line with a standard modular plug. A lamp (or lamps, up to a stated maximum) plugged into it will then flash whenever the telephone rings. For more visibility, use a colored bulb. Install several lamps or mount mirrors in the corners of the shop so you can see the light from anywhere.

—*John Seidel, Smyrna, Ga.*

TIP: Visitors won't startle you if you hook up a visual "doorbell" in your shop. Near the entrance, install a switch that controls a lamp inside the shop. Use mirrors or additional lamps if necessary for visibility. Do not use your main shop lights as the signal. Post a large sign instructing persons entering the shop to flip the switch on and off several times, and to wait to be waved in. Make sure that everyone in your household understands the danger of entering the shop unnoticed.

—*Edward DeMay, Canandaigua, N.Y.*

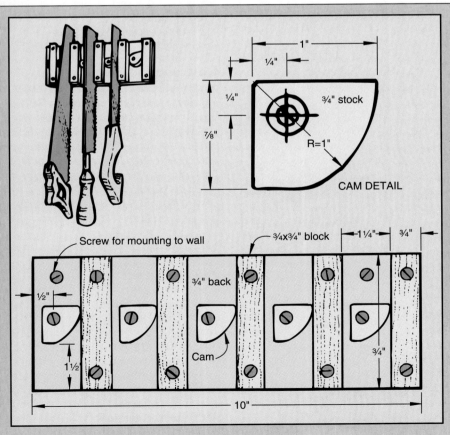

1"

¼"

¼"

7⁄8"

¾" stock

R=1"

CAM DETAIL

Screw for mounting to wall

¾x¾" block

1¼"

¾"

¾" back

½"

Cam

1½"

¾"

10"

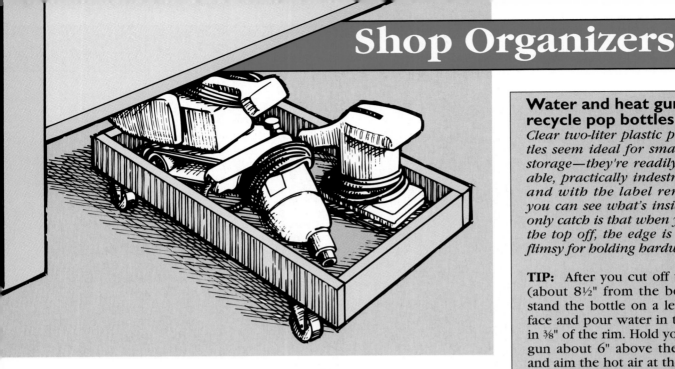

Water and heat gun recycle pop bottles

Clear two-liter plastic pop bottles seem ideal for small-parts storage—they're readily available, practically indestructible and with the label removed, you can see what's inside. The only catch is that when you cut the top off, the edge is a little flimsy for holding hardware.

TIP: After you cut off the top (about 8½" from the bottom), stand the bottle on a level surface and pour water in to within ⅜" of the rim. Hold your heat gun about 6" above the bottle and aim the hot air at the water surface. The plastic rim will curl inward, forming a sturdy lip. Want a lid? Gently heat the black plastic bottom of another bottle to soften the glue holding it on, and then twist it off. It will slip right onto the top of your new container, as shown in the drawing at *right*.

—*Anthony Quaglino, Jr., Harvey, La.*

A handy storage spot for your tools

Tools that only get occasional use don't deserve premium bench space or room on the shelves in a tight-quarters workshop. So where do you put them?

TIP: Make better use of available space by storing tools on carts that roll under your bench as shown *above*. Assemble the cart from ¾" stock for the sides, ½" plywood for the bottom, and four casters.

—*Janeil Johnson, Whitehorse, Yukon*

Color-coded outlets help prevent electrical overloads

In some workshops, more than one electrical circuit serves the convenience outlets. Still, a dust collector, a work light, and a tablesaw could pop a circuit breaker if they end up plugged into the same circuit. You need to divide your loads among circuits, not just outlets.

TIP: For each outlet on the same circuit, paint a dot of one color on the outlet plate. (Acrylic artist's colors work great for color-coding.) Identify the circuit breaker in the load center with a corresponding color dot. Designate other circuits with other colors. Now, when you plug in equipment that will be running concurrently, make sure you don't plug too much of it into outlets marked with the same color.

—*Bob Blackman, Sunrise Beach, Mo.*

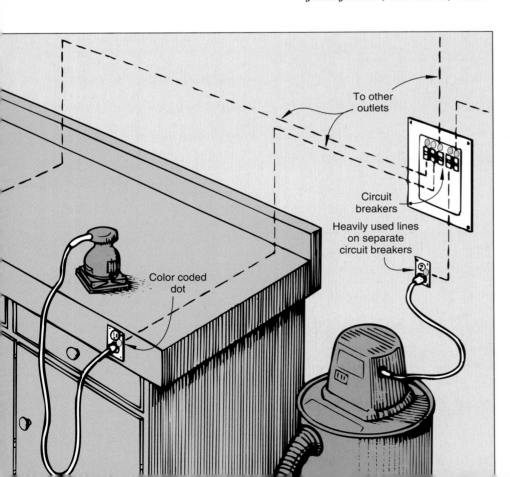

To other outlets

Circuit breakers

Heavily used lines on separate circuit breakers

Color coded dot

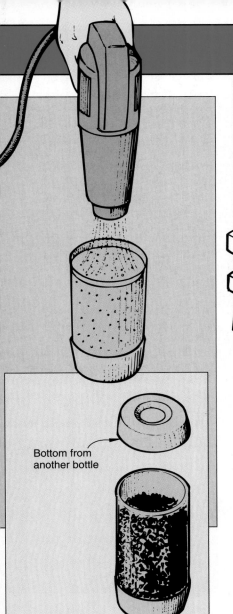

Bottom from another bottle

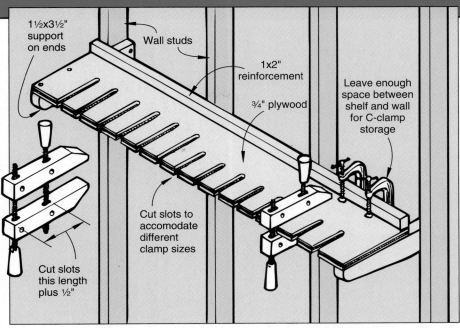

1½x3½" support on ends

Wall studs

1x2" reinforcement

¾" plywood

Leave enough space between shelf and wall for C-clamp storage

Cut slots to accomodate different clamp sizes

Cut slots this length plus ½"

Keep handscrews handy with overhead storage

Handscrew clamps, your helpers for so many shop tasks, can leave you feeling helpless when it comes time to put them away. They sure fill up a lot of storage space, fast.

TIP: For out-of-the-way, yet easy-to-reach storage, hang those handscrews high on a wall with the storage rack shown *above*. Make it out of ¾" plywood 12" wide, of a length to suit your situation.

Allow ½" spacing between clamps when you lay out the ½"-wide slots. To determine slot depth, measure from the front side of the threaded rod nearest the clamp tip to the back of the clamp and add ½". For each slot, drill a ½" hole the proper distance from the front edge of the rack, and then cut to it with a portable jigsaw. Screw and glue a 1×2" strip, on edge, to the topside of the rack at the back edge.

Mount the shelf high, using appropriate brackets. By leaving 3" between the rack and the wall, you can hook large C-clamps over the back for storage.

—*D.B. Gonzalez Jr, Pensacola, Fla.*

Photocopies make for easy reference while working

Many fantastic plans for projects appear in periodicals such as WOOD magazine, but hauling them into the shop and referring to them as you work invariably damages the pages.

TIP: Photocopy the pages with the drawings, lists and other information you need and post them near your work area. The copies can get as ratty as they like; you simply toss them when finished.

—*D. K. Bonisch,*
Wellington, New Zealand

Shop Organizers

Tin-can organizers store stuff and tote it, too

You've organized your screws, nails, and other hardware into cans. But they don't stack neatly, and you can only carry a couple at a time.

TIP: Assemble those cans into stackable, totable six-packs, as shown at *right*. Begin by connecting six cans into two rows of three (coffee cans or other large cans work best). Join them near the tops with ⅛"-long pop rivets; solder the bottoms together, or glue them with epoxy.

Next, measure your assembled cans to determine dimensions A and B. Set dimension C equal to ⅔ of A, and dimension D equal to ¾ of A. Make dimension E equal to ½ of B. Now, cut the handle from ¼" hardboard. Cut a carrying slot where shown. Attach a can assembly to each side of the handle with ½"-long pop rivets.

To make a lid, place the completed organizer on top of another piece of ¼"-thick hardboard, and draw a round-cornered rectangle around it. Center a ⁵⁄₁₆"-wide slot about ¹⁄₁₆" longer than dimension D on the lid. Cut out the lid and the slot with a scrollsaw.

—*Thomas O'Donovan*
Highland Park, Ill.

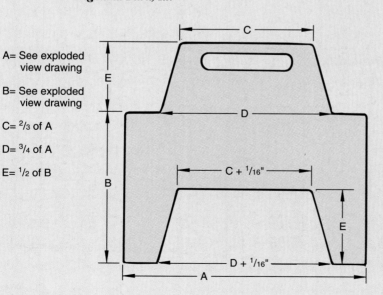

Cut slot for handle

Cut top to fit

Pop rivet tops together and to handle

Large cans

Units stack on top of each other

Epoxy or solder bottoms together

B

A

A= See exploded view drawing

B= See exploded view drawing

C= ²/₃ of A

D= ³/₄ of A

E= ¹/₂ of B

C

E

D

B

C + ¹/₁₆"

E

D + ¹/₁₆"

A

Important shop papers need organization

You'd like to refresh your memory on a couple of points before changing your jointer's knives. But the instruction book doesn't seem to be in the drawer where you remember seeing it last

TIP: Keep instructions and other important information for your tools and equipment in a binder for ready reference. Place the papers for each tool or piece of equipment into plastic document protectors (available from your local office-supply dealer) and insert them into a loose-leaf binder. Separate the sections for your various tools with tabbed divider pages. Then, label the binder and keep it on a shelf in your shop.

—*Alan Sawyer, South Portland, Maine*

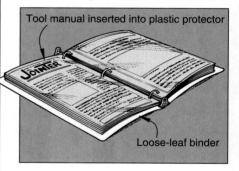

Tool manual inserted into plastic protector

Loose-leaf binder

Yes, you can organize dowel-rod odds and ends

Woodworkers usually end up with an odd assortment of dowel rods. Long pieces and short ones in many diameters defy logical organization—usually no two are alike. What's be done?

TIP: To store a lot of dowels neatly, get a couple of large, empty cans. (Restaurants or institutional kitchens often have really large ones.) Attach one to the wall about 6–12" above the floor. Cut the bottom out of the other can and mount it about 12" directly above the first one.

—*M. J. Delgado, Three Rivers, Calif.*

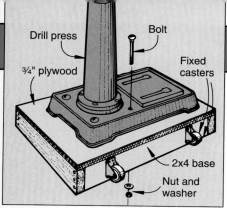

Drill press gets around on an easy-to-build base

Casters work great for moving tools. But a floor-standing drill press, with its high center of gravity, is an exception. How can you move one of these short of grabbing it in a bear hug?

TIP: Construct a base like the one shown *above* from pieces of 2×4 and ¾" plywood. Install a pair of 2" rigid-plate casters (non-swiveling) on the left side. Locate the casters so the wheels clear the floor by about ⅛". Bolt the drill press to the base.

To move the drill press, stand facing the left side of the machine and tip it slowly toward you like a two-wheel dolly. Support the drill press securely by holding onto the table or head, whichever is convenient. Tilt it just far enough for the wheels to contact the floor, and roll it away.

—*Jeff Masterson, Monterey, Calif.*

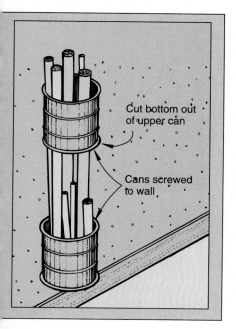

Floor-level air hose keeps a low profile

A wall-mounted retractable reel keeps your air hose handy and protects it, too. Usually, the reel hangs at benchtop height for convenience. But the convenience ends as soon as the reeled-out hose blocks your path around the shop or sweeps a stack of project parts and tools off your benchtop.

TIP: Install the hose reel at floor level. That way, when it crosses your path, you can simply step over it. To keep the hose-end handy, snap it into a conveniently located spring clip, the type used to hang brooms.

—**WOOD** *magazine's IDEA SHOP*

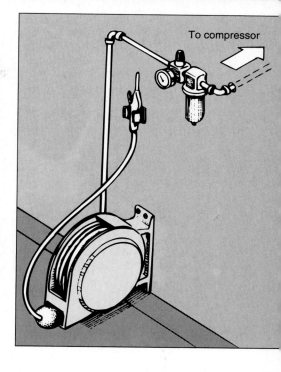

Bar clamps contribute to upstanding storage plan

Cutting sheets of plywood into large project parts can severely strain shop space. By the time you stack the uncut sheets and find a place to stack the cut pieces, you may not have much room left to do the sawing.

TIP: In a workshop with open ceiling joists, such as a garage, there's a quick answer to your storage problem. Just attach a long pipe clamp to a joist, with the pipe hanging down. Set the distance between the wall and the clamp to accommodate the material you're storing. Now you can stand the pieces on end, straight and close to the wall. When you've completed the project, take down the clamp.

—*Augie Inciong, Laguna Niguel, Calif.*

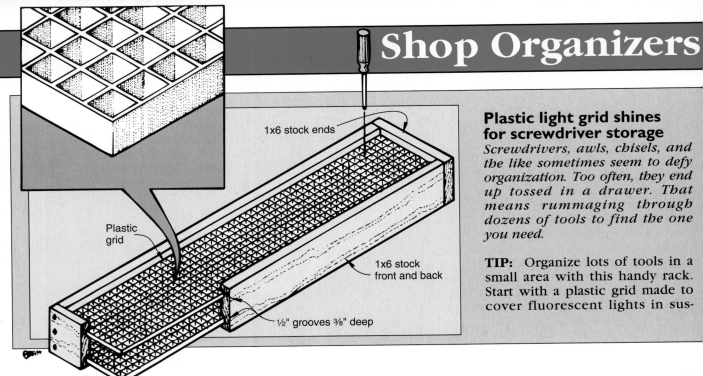

1x6 stock ends

Plastic grid

1x6 stock front and back

½" grooves ⅜" deep

Plastic light grid shines for screwdriver storage

Screwdrivers, awls, chisels, and the like sometimes seem to defy organization. Too often, they end up tossed in a drawer. That means rummaging through dozens of tools to find the one you need.

TIP: Organize lots of tools in a small area with this handy rack. Start with a plastic grid made to cover fluorescent lights in sus-

Designated drop box collects shop strays

A screwdriver ends up in the dining room after a home-repair job. A tool catalog and a couple of pamphlets lie on the coffee table in the living room. And the sanding belts you bought last weekend still occupy that corner of the kitchen counter. Not everyone in your household applauds this whole-house workshop concept, or knows exactly where to put these things away.

TIP: Build a simple tray or box (or use an existing one), and place it near the door that leads to your workshop– the basement door or the one out to the garage, for instance. Now, whoever encounters something anywhere in the workshop can drop it into the box. Whenever you head for the shop, grab the stuff out of the box to take with you.

—*Dennis Drechsler, Victoria, B.C.*

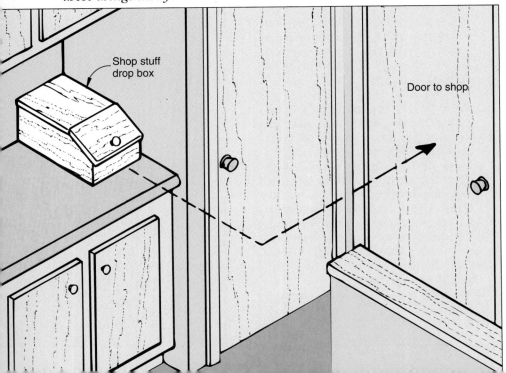

Shop stuff drop box

Door to shop

Sandwich bag

Sandwich bag locks out shop dust and moisture

A small pocket calculator comes in handy in a workshop, and some woodworkers rely on one constantly. However, wood dust, moisture, and liquid spills can play havoc with a calculator's delicate workings.

TIP: Place the calculator inside a clear, resealable sandwich bag and keep it there. You can still easily operate the calculator and read its results, without worrying about damage from dust, debris or fluids.

—*R. C. Proffitt, Oak Harbor, Wash.*

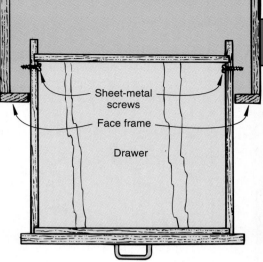

pended ceilings (available in 2×4' panels at most lumberyards and home centers). Cut two matching pieces of the grid to a convenient size.

Build the surround from 1×6" (nominal) stock. Cut ⅜"-deep grooves to hold the grids ¾" from each edge on the inside face. Assemble the surround with screws, and hang the completed rack on your toolboard or shop wall.

—Harvey Charbonneau, Ocala, Fla.

Screws prevent dumping a full drawer on the floor

A drawer without stops will unload itself all over the floor if you aren't careful when you open it. Isn't there some simple way to limit a drawer's slide?

TIP: End unplanned drawer removals by driving a screw through each side of the drawer–from the inside. Drill a pilot hole near the upper back corner of each side, and then slide the drawer a few inches into its opening. Now, drive a 1½" screw into the pilot hole (a screw with threads all the way up to the head, such as a sheet-metal screw, works best). The screw points will catch on the inside of the frame so the drawer won't slide out accidentally.

—Al VandenBoogard, Appleton, Wis.

Sheet-metal screws
Face frame
Drawer

Organize quickly with moldings and hardboard

Few things can become as cluttered as a workbench drawer. Your valuable shop time ticks away while you rummage through the jumbled up mess in your tool drawer, trying to uncover the router wrenches or some other tool you need.

TIP: Establish a separate compartment for each tool and its accessories with custom drawer dividers. Assemble them quickly with quarter-round molding, hardboard, and hotmelt glue as shown at *right*.

—Edward Kreusser, M.D., San Diego, Calif.

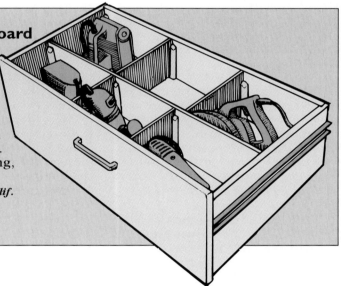

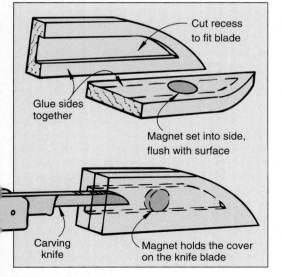

Cut recess to fit blade

Glue sides together

Magnet set into side, flush with surface

Carving knife

Magnet holds the cover on the knife blade

This knife sheath sticks to the job

When you're not carving with them, you should cover your knife blades to protect against nicks and damage—both to the blades and to your hands. You can't always find a sheath that will stay on the blade, though.

TIP: Build a scrapwood blade cover with a magnet to keep it in place. Trace around the blade on one piece of scrapwood about ⅜" thick. Carve out the marked area to accommodate the blade. Draw another line parallel to the blade outline, and about ⅜" from it. Stack the marked piece on top of another piece of stock, and scrollsaw along the line. Drill a hole in the uncarved piece, as shown in the drawing at *left*, and insert an appropriate magnet. Glue the magnet in place with epoxy or cyanoacrylate adhesive. Then, glue the two halves of the sheath together, sand, and finish.

—Leonard Wovna, Bayonne, N.J.

Radial-arm Saws

True up rough boards with clamps and straightedge

There are several techniques that enable you to cut a straight edge on a rough board using your tablesaw. But, what do you do if you have a radial-arm saw?

TIP: Set up your radial-arm saw for ripping, making sure the blade is parallel with the front edge of the table. Clamp a straightedge or guide board to the bottom of your workpiece, parallel with the cutting line and far enough from the cutting edge for stability and safety while cutting. Flip the board over and, guiding the straightedge along the front of the saw table, cut the true edge. The second edge can be cut with the regular rip fence.

—*Walter Pleier, Greenville, N.C.*

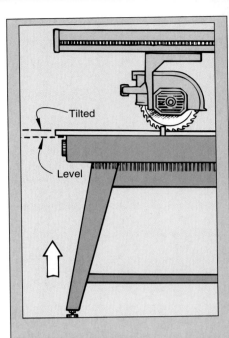

A one-minute fix for a creepy radial-arm saw

Radial-arm saws rate as one of the most dangerous machines in your shop, and they can be especially threatening if the blade carriage tends to creep forward on its own.

TIP: Tilt the machine backwards slightly by elevating the front legs as shown in the drawing *above*. If the base doesn't have pads that elevate by turning them, add a few shims.

—*David M. Johnson, New Springfield, Ohio*

Extendable stop adjusts for double duty

You can purchase or rig all sorts of cut-off stops that clamp to the fence of your radial-arm saw. But, these stops limit the length of your repetitive cuts because they extend no farther than the ends of your fence. Here's a better idea.

TIP: Build an extendable stop such as the one shown *below* for your radial-arm saw. From a ¾×1½" length of straight-grain hardwood, cut the adjustment bar to a length that suits most of your projects (mine adjusts for cuts from 0-60"). Rout a ⅜" slot through the bar, and screw an L-shaped stop to one end. Drill a 7/16" hole near the end of your fence, and secure the adjustment bar to the fence with ⅜" carriage bolt as shown in the Short Cuts and Long Cuts drawings, *below*, *left* and *right*.

—*Steve Lively, Brainerd, Minn.*

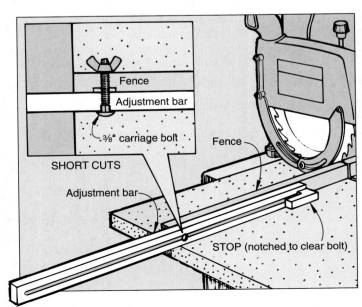

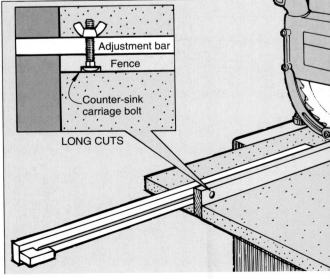

Featherboards assist in thin strip ripping

Most woodworkers cringe when it comes time to rip a thin strip from a board with a radial-arm saw. The jumping and chattering of the board and the fear of kickback make this an operation many would prefer to avoid.

TIP: A trio of featherboards can provide relief when you rip with a radial-arm saw. Make two adjustable vertical featherboards like the one shown *top left*. Then, screw one to the saw fence on each side of the blade. Adjust them to hold the workpiece down firmly while allowing you to feed it through without undue force.

Affix a third featherboard to the table to keep the board pressed against the fence. Now, rip the board using a thin-kerf carbide-tipped blade and a pushstick. This way, you'll get a cleaner cut and a less harrowing experience.

—*Charles Williams, LaCombe, La.*

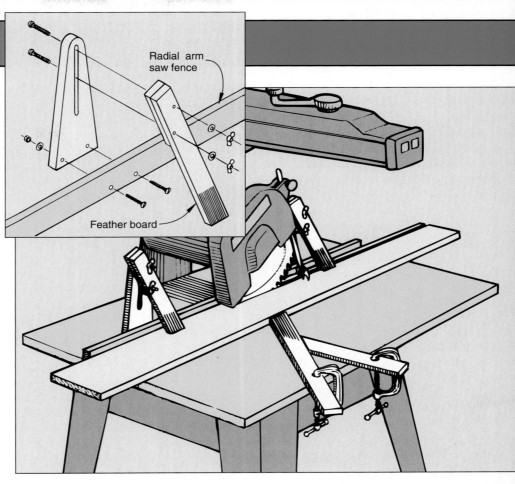

Radial arm saw fence

Feather board

Inverted fence paves way for smoother rips

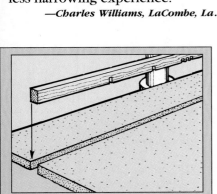

Instant panic can result from catching a corner of your stock on the fence of your radial-arm saw while making a rip. The culprit: snagging the material on one of the kerfs in the wooden fence.

TIP: Avoid this problem by loosening the fence and turning it over so the kerfs face down. When finished, be sure to return the fence to its normal position.

—*B. H. Freeman, Springfield, Va.*

Change miter angle easily with thinner table board

You need to readjust the miter angle on your radial-arm saw. Unfortunately, that means you must again raise the arm so the blade will clear the table, make your adjustment, and then lower it again. What a lot of bother!

TIP: Replace the section of the saw table behind the fence with thinner material. For a table made of 1⅟₁₆"-thick particleboard, for instance, just cut a piece of ½"-thick particleboard to fit in place of the thicker piece. (Save the piece you take out for possible future use.) With the thinner piece in place, your blade will clear the table easily without raising the arm, and you can adjust your miter angle in short order.

—*David Ryan, Columbus, Ohio*

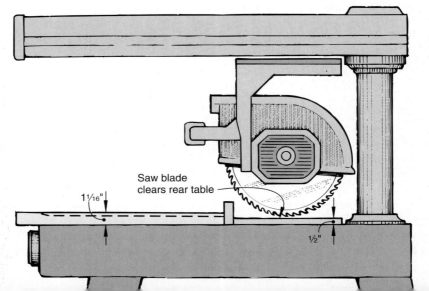

Saw blade clears rear table

1⅟₁₆"

½"

Routing

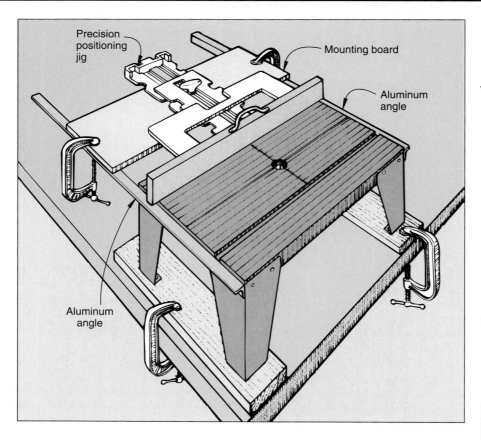

Precision positioning jig

Mounting board

Aluminum angle

Aluminum angle

Attach a fancy-joint jig to a smaller router table

You'd like to make some fancy joints by using a precision positioning jig on your router table. The only hitch is that the device is too big to fit on your table.

TIP: Attach an extension arm, as shown at *left*, to your table to hold the jig. Mount an appropriate length of ⅛"-thick 1½×1½" aluminum angle at each end of the table, extending beyond the back edge. Drill mounting holes as necessary and attach the extensions with machine screws and nuts. Now, fasten the positioning jig to a piece of wood long enough to span the extension arms, and clamp it in place. Since the router table will now be tail heavy, screw it to scrapwood and clamp it to your workbench.

—*Donald Flaig, Kenmore, N.Y.*

Router shaves edge for gap-free joint

You're troubled by gaps along the mating line between the top and bottom parts of a small box you've just completed. Is there some way to true up the mating edges without resorting to a lot of sanding or planing?

TIP: This is a job for your table-mounted router fitted with a straight bit as shown *below*. For each part, cut spacer blocks about ⅛" taller than the inside depth. Fasten them inside the part with double-faced tape. Then, place the part upside down on the router table. Adjust the router to take a light cut—about ⅟₃₂"—off the edge all around. Do the same for the other part. You'll end up with flat, true mating surfaces and a lid that fits.

—*George E. Casey, Tacoma, Wash.*

A simple guard protects against flying debris

A router table can be an indispensable tool, but if a router-bit shank breaks, look out! Any of the pieces falling into the router housing can cause extensive damage to the router's cooling fan and motor

TIP: Place a piece of fiberglass window screen over the bottom of the router to block any broken bit pieces. Small drops of cyanoacrylate (instant) glue will hold the screen in place

—*Roger Ronald, Sachse, Texas*

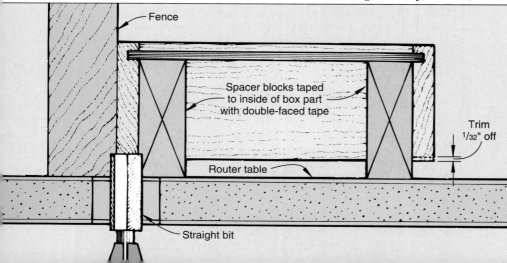

Fence

Spacer blocks taped to inside of box part with double-faced tape

Trim ⅟₃₂" off

Router table

Straight bit

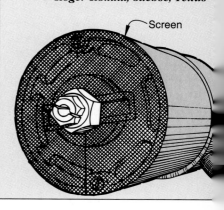

Screen

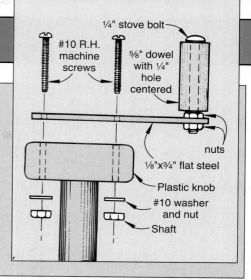

Adjust plunge router more easily with crank

You have trouble turning the slippery plastic depth-adjustment knob on your plunge router. The situation only gets worse when you mount the router upside down on the underside of your router table.

TIP: Add a crank to your router knob. Fabricate the crank from a suitable length of ⅛×¾" flat steel (a mending plate from the hardware store would work), a ¼×2½" stove bolt with two nuts, and a 2" length of ⅝"-diameter dowel. Drill a ¼" hole centered side to side near one end of the steel, then assemble the crank as shown at *right*. Attach it to the router knob with nuts and bolts or screws into threaded holes.

—Ray Macke, Marissa, Ill.

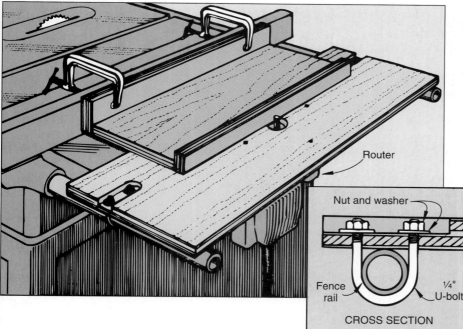

Router

Nut and washer

Fence rail

¼" U-bolt

CROSS SECTION

Router table mounts easily on tablesaw

A table-mounted router simplifies many operations, but finding space for another piece of equipment isn't always simple.

TIP: Mount your router on your tablesaw. Simply attach the router to a piece of ¾" plywood long enough to span your saw's fence guides. Secure the table to the guides with ¼" U-bolts, as shown at *left*. The router fence clamps to the saw fence for easy adjustment. Both pieces store in a small space.

—Robert Speas, Winston-Salem, N.C.

Accurate router-table depth gauge

Adjusting the depth of cut of a router bit can be a hit-or-miss proposition. The trial-and-error method can eat up a lot of time and waste a lot of scrapwood.

TIP: Build the simple depth gauge, as shown at *right,* from hardwood scraps fitted with a length of ⅜" threaded rod and two nuts. First, file the ends of the rod smooth, then bore a ⁷⁄₃₂" hole and use epoxy to attach one nut to the wooden base. On a flat surface such as a tablesaw top, turn the rod until it contacts the flat surface. Thread the second nut onto the rod until it is finger-tight against the attached nut. With epoxy, glue the second nut to the rod and file an index notch into one side. This size rod has 16 threads per inch, so one full revolution raises or lowers the rod ¹⁄₁₆". Likewise, a half-turn equals ¹⁄₃₂" and so on.

—B. W. Glass, Annandale, Va.

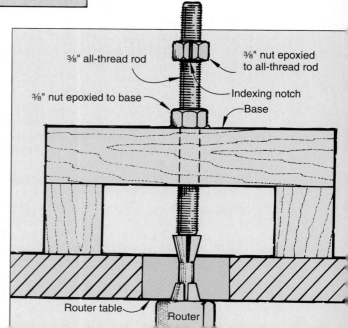

⅜" all-thread rod

⅜" nut epoxied to base

⅜" nut epoxied to all-thread rod

Indexing notch

Base

Router table

Router

Routing

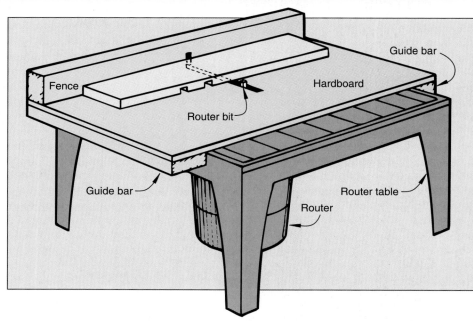

Fence

Router bit

Guide bar

Guide bar

Hardboard

Router table

Router

Sliding tabletop eases dado routing

Routing dadoes-grooves across the grain-poses several challenges, especially on narrow stock. Securing the workpiece, spacing the dadoes, and guiding the router straight over the stock become even more difficult on small workpieces.

TIP: A sliding top for your router table makes dado-routing easy. Start with a piece of ⅛"-thick tempered hardboard as wide as the front-to-back dimension of your router table and about 4" longer than the end-to-end distance.

O-ring ends "oh, darn!" when changing bit

The edge-forming router bit you're chucking keeps sliding all the way down in the collet, but it needs to be higher. With both hands occupied with collet wrenches, you can't hold the bit in position.

TIP: Slide a rubber O-ring onto the router-bit shank, as shown *below*, before you insert it into the collet. (You'll find ¼"- and ½"-inside diameter O-rings in the plumbing aisle) Position the bit at the height you want, and slide the O-ring down to the collet face. Now, you can tighten the collet nut while the O-ring holds the bit for you.

—William Sand, Morristown, Minn.

Wing nut

Washer

Reversible fence, one side notched, one side straight

Hex-head bolt

Conduit

Washers as spacers

Nut and washer

Eyebolt

Conduit

Benchtop router table

Clampless fence makes router setup fiddle-free

Fiddling with clamps for the fence each time you change your router-table setup becomes tiresome. It would sure be nice to have an adjustable fence.

TIP: Add an adjustable fence to any router table—wood or metal—using eyebolts and metal electrical conduit, as shown *above*. Cut two pieces of ½" conduit long enough to reach from end to end on your router table. Drill a ¼" hole about ¾" from each end of each piece (make

sure the holes on each end are aligned). Drill matching bolt holes or pilot holes in the router table. Slide a 5⁄16×2" eyebolt onto each conduit, and then attach the conduits to the table using washers as spacers where shown.

For the fence, cut a piece of ¾×1½" hardwood long enough to extend about 1" beyond each side. Cut a notch in each end to accept the eyebolt shank and one to clear the router bit. Tighten the fence down with a washer and wing nut on each eyebolt.

—Joe Bodi, Toledo, Ohio

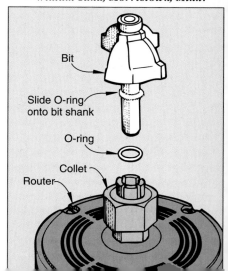

Bit

Slide O-ring onto bit shank

O-ring

Collet

Router

Attach a 1×2" guide bar across each end on the underside, locating them so the hardboard slides without excessive side play. Chuck the straight bit for dadoing into the router, and push the hardboard sliding tabletop into it, cutting a slot about halfway across the hardboard. Notch a 1×2" fence to clear the bit, and then mount it at the back of the sliding top. To rout dadoes, hold the workpiece firmly against the fence and slide the tabletop across the bit. Add stopblocks for repetitive cuts.

—C. E. Rannefeld, Decatur, Ala.

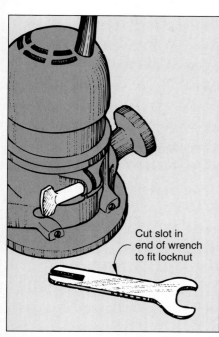

Cut slot in end of wrench to fit locknut

Cut a slot in your wrench to loosen a tough nut

You can't get enough of a grip to loosen the height-adjustment locking nut on your router.

TIP: Cut a slot in the handle of one of the collet wrenches, shown *above*. Size the slot to fit the locking nut on your router. Now, you won't have to resort to pliers—the right tool will always be near at hand.

—*Jack E. Battalia, M.D., Portland, Ore.*

Simple hold-down gives tip-up the brush-off

Long stock can be hard to handle on a router table. The overhanging end tends to tip the other end away from the bit.

TIP: Cut two 1×4" crossbars to span the router table front to back. Then, from stock the same thickness as the workpiece, cut four spacers 2–4" wide, and about 6" long. Clamp to the table as shown, placing a ¹⁄₃₂"-thick shim between each crossbar and spacer. Secure the router table so that the weight of the extra-long workpiece won't upset it.

—*Honest John Adams*

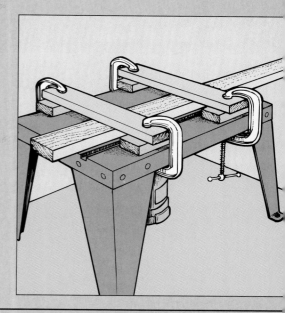

Paint filter keeps router innards clean

Your table-mounted router sucks in a lot of sawdust under the table. You'd like to help it breathe a little cleaner air.

TIP: Affix a bag-type painter's strainer to the top of the router motor housing. Cut a hole for the cord, and secure the bag to the router with a wide rubber band. It helps to drop a small piece of scrapwood into the nylon-mesh bag to keep it extended. Shake the dust off the bag occasionally so it won't clog and cut off air flow.

—*Bruce Buckingham, Mt. Pleasant, Iowa*

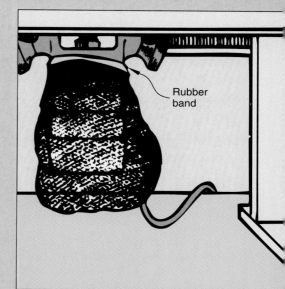

Rubber band

Nail set knocks a stubborn bit out of its collet

When trying to change router bits, the old one won't come out of the collet. You can't get enough of a grip on either piece to get them apart.

TIP: Hold a nail set against your benchtop with the tip pointing up. Then, put the open bottom of the collet over the nail set and push against the router-bit shank. Tap the shank end against the nail set until the bit breaks loose.

—*from the WOOD magazine shop*

Nail set

Routing

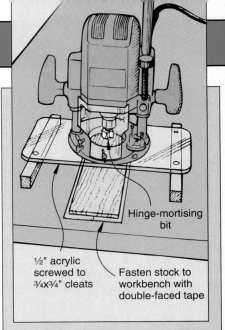

Multiple-pass cuts go quickly with spacers

You like to make certain cuts with your table-mounted router in steps, cutting a little deeper each time. What you don't like is reaching under the table to adjust the router 1/16" or 1/8" after each cut—it sure slows down the job.

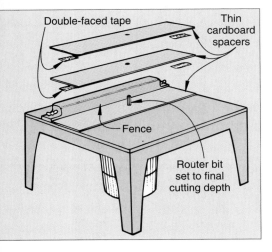

Double-faced tape

Thin cardboard spacers

Fence

Router bit set to final cutting depth

TIP: Set your router to the final cut depth, and then leave it there. Now, make your depth adjustments by laying several pieces of thin cardboard, artist's mat board, or poster board (all available from art-supply dealers and some crafts shops), or even 1/8" hardboard on the router table. Each piece must be wide enough and extend far enough past the bit on each side to support your workpiece properly. Cut a hole in each piece for the router bit to protrude through, and secure the pieces to the table with double-faced tape.

Make your first cut with all of the shims stacked in place. Remove one for each subsequent pass until you've removed them all for the final cut. Each one you remove increases your depth of cut by its thickness.

—Bob Agner, Muskego, Wis.

Hinge-mortising bit

1/2" acrylic screwed to 3/4x3/4" cleats

Fasten stock to workbench with double-faced tape

Router stands in for a surface planer

You need a small piece of thin stock for a project, but not enough to justify the cost of a planer. Or, maybe you have a planer, but the piece you need to plane down is just too short to run safely through the machine. Are resawing or hand-planing your only choices?

TIP: Put your router on the job with an easy-to-build elevated base, shown *above*. Bore a 2" hole through the center of a piece of clear polycarbonate plastic or plywood as wide as your router's base and about twice as long. Attach the router over the hole on top of the piece with the handles aligned lengthwise. On the bottom, attach a 1×1×12" strip centered across each end.

Fasten the workpiece to a saw table or other flat, smooth surface with double-faced tape. Use plenty of tape, and tap the face of the wood lightly with a non-marring mallet to ensure a tight bond. Now, with a hinge-mortising bit in the router, adjust the depth of cut to skim off enough material to leave the thickness you need. If you need to remove a lot of material, take it off in small increments.

—William Kappele, Mission Viejo, Calif.

Long arm lends hand when trimming edges

You can't rout assembled box or drawer edges very well, especially inside edges, with a hand-held router. The narrow edge doesn't support the router properly, so you end up with a poor cut. A table-mounted router does the job, but what if you don't have one, or the work is too cumbersome to handle on a table?

TIP: Build an extended base for your router from 1/4" plywood and 3/4" hardwood, as shown *below*. The plywood width should equal your router-base diameter. Make it long enough to span your project.

Round one end using the router base as a template, and mark the mounting holes and router-bit opening. Then, drill the opening for the router bit. Drill and countersink the mounting-screw holes. Cut the hardwood stiffening spine, and then glue and screw it into place. Mount the router to your new extended base, and you're ready to tackle those outside or inside edges with ease.

—Ken Seals, Edenton, N.C.

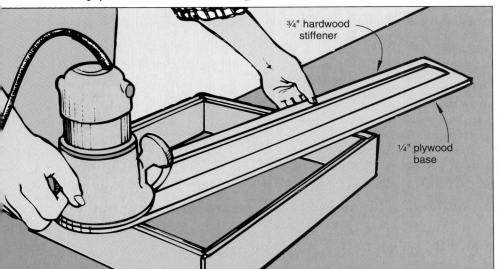

3/4" hardwood stiffener

1/4" plywood base

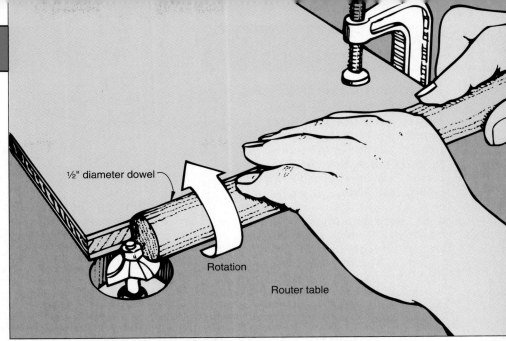

Use a router to enlarge wide-diameter holes

A drill press and Forstner bit or circle cutter work great for boring holes with diameters exceeding 1". However, if the workpiece doesn't fit on the drill-press table, that approach won't work.

TIP: Locate the center of the hole to be drilled, and with a compass, scribe its circumference on the surface opposite the faceside. Next, bore a hole of the desired size in a scrap of ¾"-thick stock. Then, center the hole over the scribed circle and attach it to the workpiece with double-faced tape or clamps as shown *below*. Drill a starter hole large enough to accept a flush trimmer bit for your router and cut the final hole.

—*Bruce L. Hasslinger,*
San Diego, Calif.

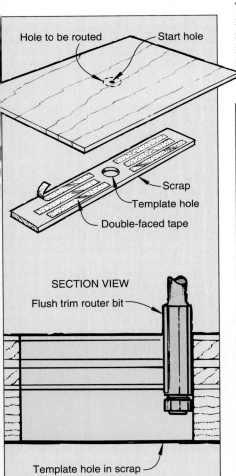

Set up a router to zip round-overs on dowels

Sanding round-overs on several dowel ends can be a trying task, especially when you want the round-overs to match.

TIP: Do the job with your table-mounted router. With a piloted round-over bit of appropriate radius in the router, set the depth as you would for rounding-over any edge. Then, clamp a fence to the table with the distance to the center of the bit equal to ½ the dowel's diameter, as shown in the drawing *above*. Turn on the router, and then slide the dowel along the fence into the bit. Rotate the dowel to form a perfect round-over.

—*from the WOOD magazine shop*

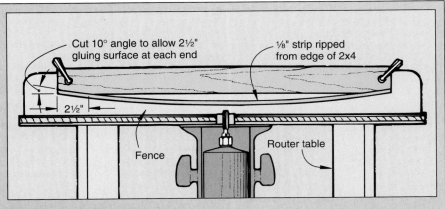

Bend a strip to hold work flat

To make a good cut with a table-mounted router, you must hold the work down firmly. Doing that without getting your fingers into the danger zone can be difficult if not impossible, particularly with an irregular workpiece.

TIP: Build a springy hold-down like the one shown *above*. Rip a ⅛" strip off the edge of a 24" length of 2×4. Cut a 10° angle at each end of the 2×4 where shown, and then glue on the strip to form an arch. The curved strip will press against your workpiece, holding it down firmly while you rout it.

—*Bruce Graham, Bennington, Kan.*

Safety

Sump-pump switch keeps hands free at drill press

Some drill-press operations require both hands, making it difficult to flip the switch, particularly in an emergency. And, looking away from the work to find the switch could cause an accident.

TIP: Put a foot-operated control on your drill press. Install a sump-pump switch (available from plumbing-supply dealers) on the machine's base. Mount the switch where it will be easy to reach with your foot but won't be turned on accidentally.

—Raymond Matthews, Port Clinton, Ohio

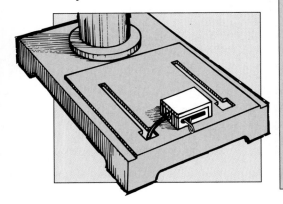

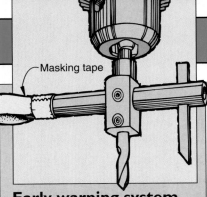

Masking tape

Early warning system for circle cutters

The swinging arm of a circle cutter is hard to see and can inflict serious injuries to fingers and hands

TIP: Applying a bright-colored paint to the ends of the arm makes it more visible and somewhat less hazardous. But for an added margin of safety, attach a loop of masking tape that extends an inch or two from the end of the arm. If your hand wanders into the path of this loop, it will smack you as a warning that you are getting too close. Also remember to operate your circle cutter no faster than 500 rpm.

—Bud Borneman
North Ridgeville, Ohio

Gather safety equipment around the door

No shop should be without a first-aid kit and a fire extinguisher. But they're useless if you, or those who might help you in an emergency, can't find them quickly.

TIP: Mount your first-aid kit and fire extinguisher where you'll see them every time you enter and leave the shop–right next to the main entrance. Keep a flashlight with the safety equipment, too, in case a power failure leaves you in the dark. And if a fire could prevent you from reaching the main entrance or trap you in a corner, install one or more additional fire extinguishers throughout the shop. In the WOOD magazine IDEA SHOP, we also have a phone by the door, along with a list of emergency numbers.

—WOOD magazine's IDEA SHOP

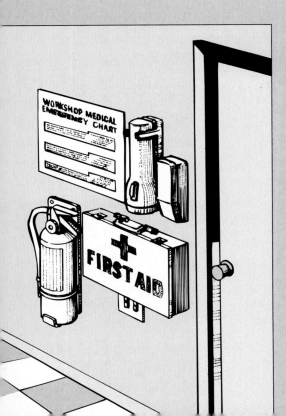

Multiple cuts go faster with a step on the table

Even with a stopblock on your mitersaw fence, making repetitive cuts takes time. You have to make the cut, wait for the blade to stop to safely remove the piece, and then slide the stock over to saw again.

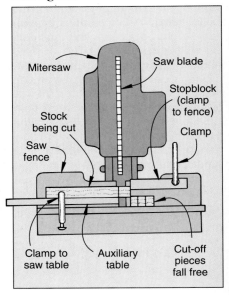

Mitersaw · Saw blade · Stopblock (clamp to fence) · Stock being cut · Clamp · Saw fence · Clamp to saw table · Auxiliary table · Cut-off pieces fall free

TIP: Speed things up and make the job safer at the same time by adding an auxiliary table and high-mounted stopblock as shown *above*. Clamp the ¾"-thick auxiliary table (plywood or particleboard will work fine) to the mitersaw table, and saw the end. Mark your stock where you wish to cut. Align that mark with the side of the blade opposite the auxiliary table. Position the stopblock against the upper corner of the stock to be cut, and clamp it to the mitersaw fence.

Now, the cut-off piece will fall to the saw table. Then, as you slide the stock to the stopblock for the next cut, it pushes the piece out of the way. With this setup, the cut piece cannot bind between the stopblock and the blade as the saw returns. And because sawdust won't build up against the stopblock, you won't end up with undersized pieces.

—Harlan Flock, Long Beach, Calif.

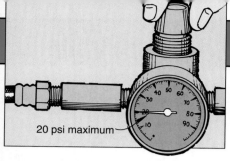

20 psi maximum

How to safely give yourself a pressurized dusting

Most woodworkers leave their compressors set in the 50-90 psi range for a variety of jobs, including dusting off themselves. However, at these high pressures, the air can get into cuts and other wounds and lift up skin. Ouch!

TIP: Remember to dial down the pressure to about 20 psi when blowing dust from your skin. At this pressure you'll still remove most of the dust, but safely. Post a sign to remind yourself.

—*Mike Atkins, Shell Beach, Calif.*

Color-coded cords end disconnection confusion

You want to unplug your drill, which is plugged into a power strip along with three other tools. So far, you've unplugged two cords without hitting the right one. It's sure hard to trace those tangled cords.

TIP: With a stripe of paint or colored plastic tape around the tool end of the cord and a corresponding strip at the plug end, you'll spot the right plug in an instant. Mark each tool (and your extension cords, too) with a different color or combination of colors. The color code also makes it easier to pick the right plug from a jumble when you want to connect a tool.

—*Gail Traynor, Riverside, Calif.*

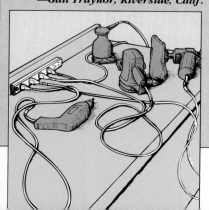

Double-duty sanding/pushblock

Safety-conscious woodworkers really appreciate pushblocks, especially when surfacing stock on a jointer. A slight modification to this accessory helps it serve other shop tasks.

TIP: Cut a sheet of sandpaper to fit your pushblock and secure the abrasive with a strip of hardwood and self-tapping screws. I use a Shopsmith pushblock, two 1/4×1/2×3" hardwood strips, and 3/4" screws. A half-sheet of paper (3½×9") fits perfectly. You can sand comfortably and leave the paper on for a better grip when using the tool as a pushblock.

—*Robert Maurice, Hartford, Wis.*

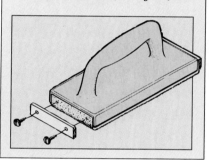

Pivoting protector keeps molding head under cover

You can do a lot with a molding head and cutters on your tablesaw. One thing you can't do, though, is put the blade guard in place to protect your fingers.

TIP: Make a jointer-type pivoting guard of 1/4"-thick clear acrylic, shown at *right*. Cut a curved edge where shown on a 6×8" piece of acrylic (or one large enough to cover your cutter) with a scrollsaw or bandsaw. Sand the curve smooth. Bolt the guard to a piece of 2"-wide stock the length of your saw table and thick enough to clear your molding cutter. Attach a rubber band where shown. Clamp the guard assembly to the saw table so that the guard rests against the saw's rip fence and over the cutter.

—*Gerald Spalla, Canonsburg, Pa.*

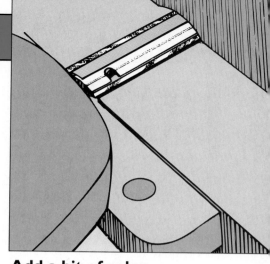

Add a bit of color for safe jointing

Since you always have the blade guard in place on your jointer, you may not give much thought to the spinning cutterhead with its sharp knives. But it's right there, almost at your fingertips.

TIP: Stick strips of yellow plastic tape to the cutterhead between the blades. Then, whenever you see a flash of yellow between your workpiece and the guard, think of the knives. Unplug the machine and clean the head before applying the tape.

—*Harold Thomson, Raytown, Mo.*

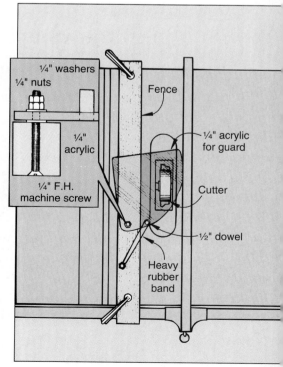

1/4" washers
1/4" nuts
1/4" acrylic
1/4" F.H. machine screw
Fence
1/4" acrylic for guard
Cutter
1/2" dowel
Heavy rubber band

Sanding

Reinforced sandpaper sticks to job longer

Hand-sanding curved edges often tears the sandpaper to tatters long before the abrasive wears out. The paper lasts longer with a sanding block, but you need flexibility.

TIP: Stick plastic package-sealing tape to the back of your sandpaper. It will then have the strength to take on the rough spots and sharp edges while remaining flexible enough to take the curves.

—*John Walsh, Martinez, Ga.*

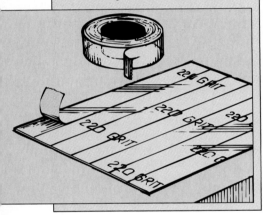

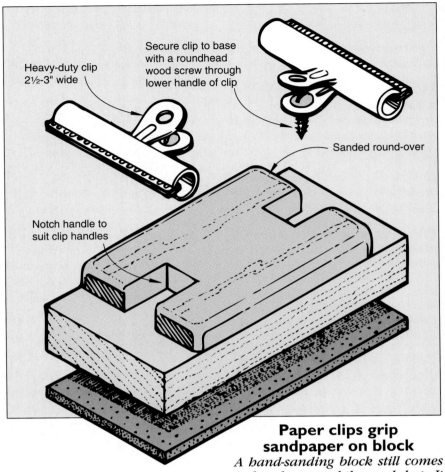

Heavy-duty clip 2½-3" wide

Secure clip to base with a roundhead wood screw through lower handle of clip

Sanded round-over

Notch handle to suit clip handles

Paper clips grip sandpaper on block

A hand-sanding block still comes in handy around the workshop. It sure would be nice to have one that allows quick and easy sandpaper changes.

TIP: Incorporate spring-type paper clips into your sanding block for a sure, simple sandpaper holder. Purchase a pair of clips 2½–3" wide. Build a sanding block from two pieces of scrapwood as shown *above*. This block uses ⅓ of a standard sheet of sandpaper. Alter the dimensions to make blocks for other sizes.

—*Rene Stebenne, Whitinsville, Mass.*

Tennis ball lobs time off sanding bowls

Sanding the inside of a turned bowl can be a tricky task. Holding sandpaper with your fingers works, but the paper soon gets hot and your hands quickly tire.

TIP: Wrap sandpaper around a tennis ball and use the combination as a sanding block. It's quick, comfortable, and easy to control.

—*John T. Schulte, Temecula, Calif.*

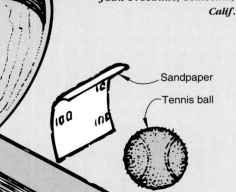

Sandpaper

Tennis ball

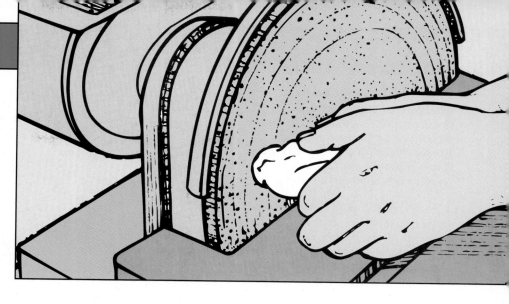

Dried-up silicone caulk cleans up abrasive

That partial tube of silicone caulk from last fall set up. Now, you have a big chunk of cured caulk that you may as well throw away.

TIP: While you can't stop drafts and leaks with it any longer, that caulk can still serve you in the shop. Strip away the tube and clean your abrasive belts or discs with the solidified silicone.

—*Robert Thompson, Buckeye Lake, Ohio*

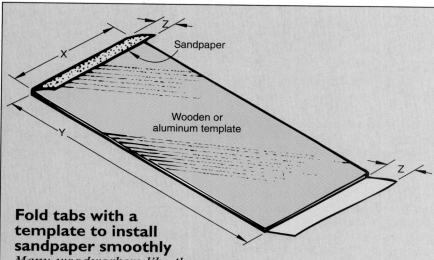

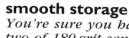

Fold tabs with a template to install sandpaper smoothly

Many woodworkers like the economy of drum sanders that use strips of sandpaper. But sizing and installing those strips drives a lot of us crazy.

TIP: Cut a piece of sandpaper to the width of the drum (dimension X on the drawing). Make it long enough to fit around the drum (dimension Y) and to allow for a clamping tab on each end (dimension Z). (This may take some time and some fiddling.) Then, make a template X-wide and Y-long out of wood or aluminum. Write on it the total length of sandpaper needed (Y plus the two tabs).

Now, whenever you need to replace the sandpaper, just cut an X-wide piece to the total length, center the template on back of it, and bend up the ends into tabs.

—*Elliott Bloom, Miami, Fla.*

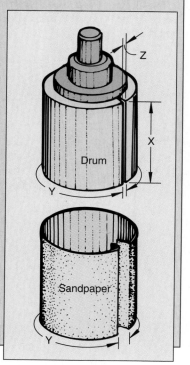

File this under smooth storage

You're sure you had a sheet or two of 180-grit sandpaper somewhere. But you can't find one in the stack of dog-eared sheets you dug out of the drawer.

TIP: Organize sandpaper the way you organize other pieces of paper--in a file. An inexpensive plastic file case with tabbed dividers makes a great storage box for sandpaper. File each grit in a separate file folder, and then you'll be able to see at a glance what you have. A letter-size case holds full sheets, while the 5×8" size works great for ¼" sheets.

—*Gary Zeff, Rancho Santa Fe, Calif.*

Sanding

Flat-sand easily with a couple of clipboards

Because small parts are difficult to hold flat against a moving abrasive, it's all too easy to round their edges or grind them to wedges when power-sanding.

TIP: Move the part over the sandpaper instead of the other way around. Place two clipboards together as shown at *right*, and clamp a sheet of sandpaper under the clips. Firmly held at both ends, the sandpaper stays smooth as you move the part back and forth to sand it flat.

—*Frank Toroney, Glenmoore, Penn.*

Clamp board ensures a sandpaper bond that keeps on holding on

Self-adhesive sanding discs and those that require spray-on adhesive can come loose or buckle after little use. For most adhesives, it helps to hold the sanding disc firmly in place against the sanding plate for a day or so as the glue sets.

TIP: Cut a circular piece of ¾" plywood the same size as the sanding disc. After applying the sandpaper, clamp the plywood to the mounting plate to press the sandpaper securely in place. Leave the plywood disc attached for at least a day to ensure a solid grip, as shown *below*. If you can't remove the sanding table, or a dust chute obstructs the bottom half of the disc, cut the clamp board in half. Then, apply the board to the top half of the disc for one day, remove the board, rotate the disc 180°, and apply the plywood to the other half of the disc.

—*Philip Cole, Ware, Mass.*

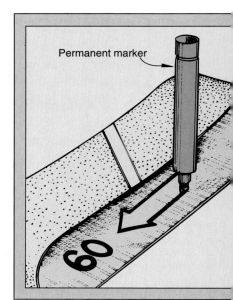

Permanent marker

60

Cornstarch prevents sticky sanding drums

Drum sanders save a lot of time in the shop. You lose a lot of that saved time, though, when you have to change the sleeve and it's stuck to the rubber drum.

TIP: Sprinkle a little cornstarch on the rubber sanding drum before you put on the sleeve. Cornstarch prevents the two sticking together, so sleeve changes are easy.

—*Al Lantinen, Portsmouth, N.H.*

Spray glue helps sandpaper stand up to machine use

Plain sandpaper doesn't last very long on your finishing sander. It wrinkles and tears and slips loose from the clamps.

TIP: Apply spray adhesive to the back of the sandpaper. When it dries, you'll have sticky sandpaper that won't slide around on the sander pad, yet will be easy to remove. To save time, prepare the sheets in batches. Stack them interleaved with pieces of waxed paper to keep the sandpaper from sticking together.

—Frank Pellicone, North East, Md.

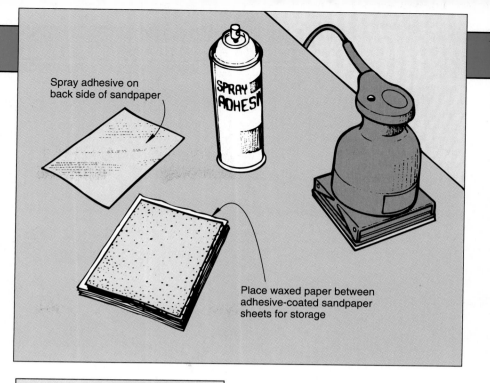

Spray adhesive on back side of sandpaper

Place waxed paper between adhesive-coated sandpaper sheets for storage

Mark your sanding belts for future reference

A sanding belt's directional and grit markings usually wear off long before the belt's abrasive does. This poses problems when you switch belts.

TIP: Before you install a new belt, add your own markings on the inside with a permanent marker—a red one works great. Draw bold directional arrows and write the grit size in large numbers. The red remains readable for a long time. You'll likely use up the belt before the markings disappear.

—Sam Chandler, Milledgeville, Ga.

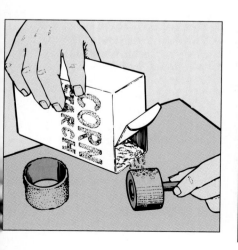

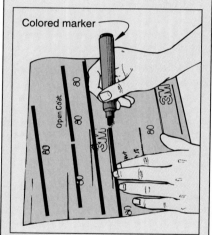

Colored marker

Colors denote grit on cut-up sandpaper

When you cut a sheet of sandpaper into smaller pieces, you can bet several won't have the grit number on the back. That makes it tough to pick the one you need.

TIP: Before you cut the sheet, scribble a crosshatch pattern on the back with a colored marker. Each cut piece then will have colored lines on the back. Use a different color for each grit, and make a color-key chart to keep with the sandpaper. Then, you can identify the grit readily.

—Daniel Angert, Orlando, Fla.

Use dull scrollsaw blades to sand difficult areas

Sometimes, you just can't get into a tight curve or follow an irregular edge very well when sanding.

TIP: Grab an old, dull scrollsaw blade and a piece of sandpaper about three-fourths the length of the blade and two inches wide. Wrap it tightly on the blade and secure the ends with thin strips of plastic electrical tape. Use it for hand-sanding, or if you really have some smoothing to do, put the blade into the scrollsaw and use it as a power sander for tight places.

—Chris Lyles, Hereford, Texas

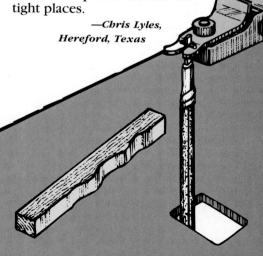

Sanding

Super-fine sandpaper puts polish on project

You've sanded your project carefully with 600-grit paper but the wood still doesn't feel quite as smooth as you'd like.

TIP: Try some finer-grit sandpaper for a super-smooth surface. 3M Imperial Wet-or-dry Color Sanding Paper, which is available from automotive-paint suppliers, comes in 1,000-, 1,200-, 1,500-, and even 2,000-grit. You'll sand your way to a fabulously smooth finish, even with one of the middle grades of paper.

—*John Hermeling, Centrali, Ill.*

Tablesaw sanding disc

A good stationary disc sander can turn the drudgery of sanding into a comparatively easy job. But, if you can't afford one, get ready for tedious hours of sanding.

TIP: Cut an 8" circle out of ¼" tempered hardboard and bore a hole the size of your tablesaw's arbor in the exact center (usually ⅝"). Use spray adhesive to attach 80-grit sandpaper to one side and 100-grit to the other. Mount the disc in place of the tablesaw blade.

CAUTION: Tablesaws run at about 4,000 rpm, so limit the use of this sanding disc to small touch-up jobs. Also, avoid standing in line with the spinning disc.

—*James L. DeSbaney, Appleton, Wis.*

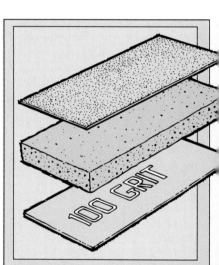

A cheap-to-make flexible sanding pad

When sanding contoured surfaces such as dowels or chair legs, a flexible sanding pad helps you reach all kinds of nooks and crannies, and doesn't wear out as fast as plain sandpaper. But, the commercially available models cost a buck or two.

TIP: You can save some of your hard-earned money by attaching 2½×4½" sheets of sandpaper to similar-sized pieces of carpet-underlay foam as shown above. I put sheets of differing grits on each side of the pad, and secure them with spray adhesive.

—*Ray Sweeney, Elizaville, N.Y.*

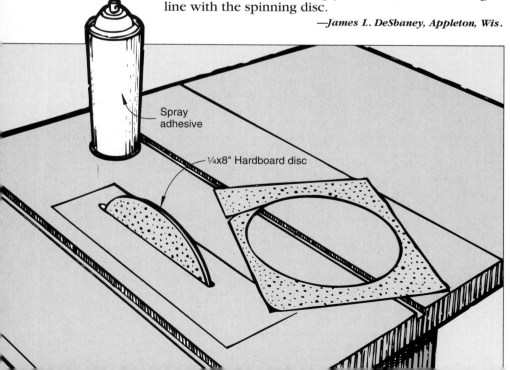

Spray adhesive

¼x8" Hardboard disc

Piece of pipe makes button sanding a cinch

Wooden buttons often need to be sanded before use. But it's sure tempting to stick them into place without sanding because they're so hard to hang on to.

TIP: Push the stem of the button into the end of a piece of copper or plastic pipe about 12" long to give yourself a better grip. Try different sizes of pipe and tubing for various buttons.

—*Mark Good, Orinda, Calif.*

Button

Pipe

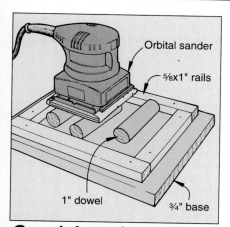

Orbital sander

⅝x1" rails

1" dowel

¾" base

Corral those dowels when sanding time rolls around

You've cut some short dowels for toy parts. Now you need to sand them, a chore that's slow-going.

TIP: From scrapwood a little more than half the thickness of your dowels (⅝–¾" thick if you're sanding 1" dowels,), cut two 1"-wide strips about 12" long and two a little longer than your dowels. Arrange the strips on a base of plywood as shown *above*, and tack them down. Now, round up your dowels and corral a few at a time inside the fence. Turn on your orbital finishing sander and roll it back and forth on the dowels. The fence strips will keep the dowels from getting away as you sand them quickly and effectively.

—*Frederick Koster, Yorktown Heights, N.Y.*

Make sanding blocks for any shape

Most power sanders were designed for working flat surfaces. But, when you must sand in tight places, these tools just don't cut it.

TIP: Convert scrap into sanding blocks of virtually any shape by covering them with 3M Stikit, an adhesive-backed sandpaper sold in rolls. Besides the shapes suggested in the drawing, adhering the abrasive material to a putty knife or even your finger often provides the shape of sanding block you need. If the abrasive peels off, staple it onto the backside or edges of the block.

—*Harold Howting, London, Ontario*

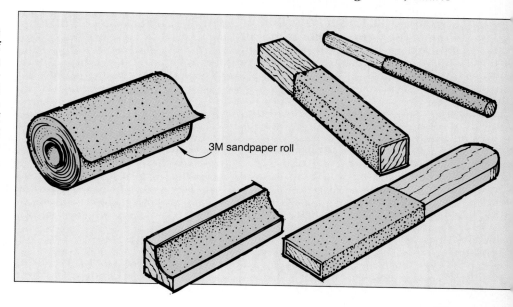

3M sandpaper roll

Scrollsaws

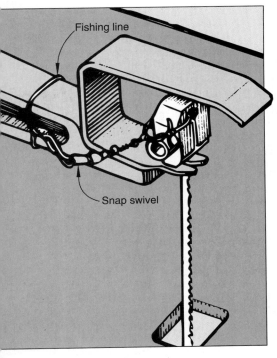

Fishing line

Snap swivel

Fishing line lands flying blade holders

Blade holders on some scroll-saws fly far and wide whenever you break a blade. Then you end up looking for the holders in the sawdust on your hands and knees. Also, a flying blade holder could hurt someone.

TIP: Put those holders on a leash. Attach a fisherman's snap swivel to each blade holder with 4-lb. test monofilament fishing line. Tie a length of line with a loop in one end to the upper saw arm and another to the lower arm. Keep the lines short so they won't tangle in the saw or work-piece. Then, with the blade and holders installed, clip the snap swivels to the loops and saw without fretting.

—*George Weber, Brooklyn, N.Y.*

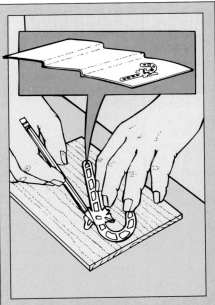

Vinyl siding scraps make lifetime scrollsaw patterns

You can trace around card-board patterns to make copies of your favorite scrollsaw cutouts. But the cardboard doesn't last very long in the workshop.

TIP: Cut your patterns from scraps of vinyl house siding instead. It's thin, cuts easily with your scrollsaw, and stands up to a lot of abuse. You can glue a photocopy or paper pattern to it, or draw on it with pencils, markers, or pens. And you can probably get all you need free from a contractor's scrap pile (but, ask first).

—*John Schwartz, Olney, Ill.*

Scrollsaw dust blower springs back into action

On some scrollsaws, the plastic tubing connecting the bellows to the dust-blower nozzle can kink. This restricts air flow, reducing the blower's usefulness.

TIP: Slide a spring from an old ballpoint pen into the tubing. Push it in far enough that the spring's middle falls at the middle of the curve where the kink occurs. The spring will prevent the tubing from collapsing, so you'll have full air flow to keep your pattern line clear.

—*Paul Backer, Mason City, Iowa*

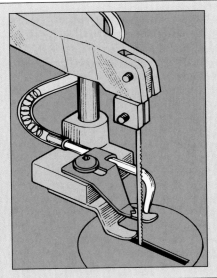

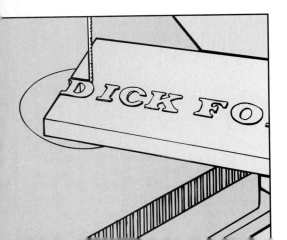

Scrollsawing small letters

Stencils and templates work fine as guides for scrollsawing 1" or larger letters, but not so well for smaller letters, if you can find them. Accurately marking small-er letters with a pencil and follow-ing those layout lines with your scrollsaw can prove taxing.

TIP: Purchase vinyl press-on let-ters from office-supply or art stores. The letters are very inex-pensive and come in many differ-ent sizes, styles, and colors. Once applied to the wood, your scroll-saw blade can follow the outline of these letters easier than you can split a pencil line. To remove the vinyl, gently lift the letters with an X-acto knife, or sand the surface of the letters after mount-ing them to a workpiece.

—*Dick Foxworthy, Widefield, Colo.*

Dowels stack up well in scrollsaw cutting

By stacking several blanks and putting a pattern on top, you can scrollsaw duplicate pieces quickly. But, how do you hold the stack together? Nails or screws could split thin stock or scratch the saw table. Double-faced tape can be troublesome to remove.

TIP: The answer: Dowels. Stack the blanks as usual and drill a hole the size of your dowel (⅛" works fine) through the waste at one corner of the stack. Drive in a piece of dowel a little shorter than the height of the stack. Repeat the process at the other corners.

—*Norman Bartlett, Peoria, Ill.*

An answer for loose scrollsaw-blade pins

Many woodworkers prefer pin-type scrollsaw blades because they mount so quickly and easily. Unfortunately, the pins occasionally work themselves loose from the blades.

TIP: Add a drop of Locktite or cyanoacrylate (instant) glue to each side of the pin and allow it to dry overnight. That's it—no more loose pins to worry about.

—*R. I. Smith, Halifax, Nova Scotia*

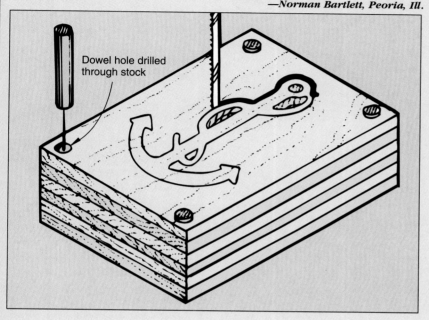

Dowel hole drilled through stock

Slot lends new life to scrollsaw screws

Lots of scrollsaws employ allen-head screws to clamp the blade holders onto the blade ends. Repeated loosening and tightening wears out the hex-shaped recess in the clamp-screw head, making it impossible to tighten the blade clamp sufficiently with an allen wrench.

TIP: Cut a slot in the clamp-screw head. A hacksaw with two blades or hand-held rotary tool with a narrow grinding wheel will do the job in short order. When you're done, you'll have a blade clamp you can tighten and loosen with an ordinary screwdriver.

—*Robert T. Hernandez, Krebs, Okla.*

Safety pin facilitates inside scrollsaw cuts

Scrollsaws that accept only pin-end blades limit your ability to make inside cuts—sometimes the smallest hole that the blade will fit through is larger than the area you want to cut out.

TIP: Remove the pin from the top of the blade. Now, raid the sewing drawer to find a heavy safety pin that fits the hole snugly. Snip the safety pin where shown. You now have a blade retaining pin with a loop handle, and a blade that fits through a much smaller start hole.

—*Gloria Massey, Spartanburg, S.C.*

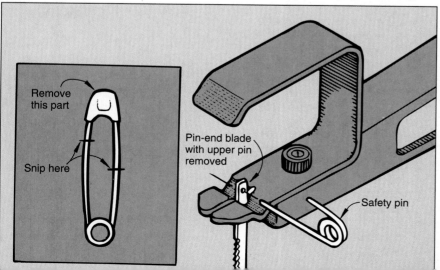

Remove this part

Snip here

Pin-end blade with upper pin removed

Safety pin

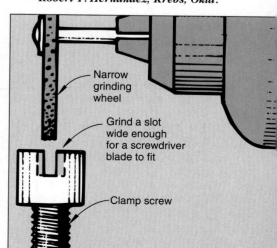

Narrow grinding wheel

Grind a slot wide enough for a screwdriver blade to fit

Clamp screw

Scrollsaws

Reinforced stock keeps scrollsaw cutouts together

When scrollsawing silhouettes from thin solid stock, small pieces break off all too easily. Even a zero-clearance table insert can't prevent all of the breakage.

TIP: Before you start cutting, cover the back of your stock with self-adhesive shelf paper or plastic packaging tape. The backing will help prevent breakage while sawing and damage later when you put the delicate cutout on display.

—*Susan Evarts, Meriden, Conn.*

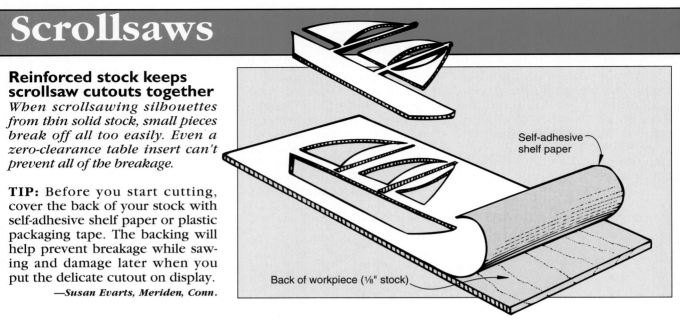

Self-adhesive shelf paper

Back of workpiece (⅛" stock)

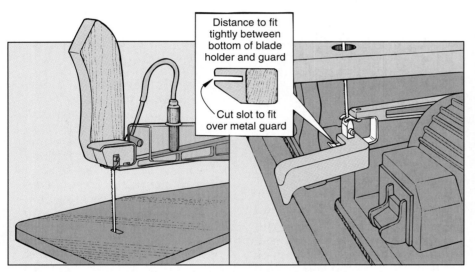

Distance to fit tightly between bottom of blade holder and guard

Cut slot to fit over metal guard

Shop-made tools end inside-cutting grief

The blade holders on some scrollsaws make every inside cut a nightmare. It's easy enough to thread the blade through a starting hole, But fitting it into the upper blade holder, and then trying to hold everything in position while you tighten the clamp screw can make you wish you'd taken up knitting instead.

TIP: You won't shy away from inside cuts after you make the shop aids shown *above*. (The ones in the drawing fit an AMT 4601 scrollsaw, but you can adapt them to other machines with similar blade holders.) Cut the parts from ¾" maple. Cut out block (A), working by trial and error to achieve a tight fit around the upper blade holder. Next, cut out the handle (B). Glue A to it, and clamp. Then, cut out the lower blade holder support (C).

To use this handy device, loosen the tension on the saw blade, and then insert the upper tool. Loosen the clamp screw, and remove the blade from the upper holder (leaving the lower blade holder attached). Feed the blade through the start hole from the bottom, insert the end into the upper holder, and install the lower blade-holder support. Tighten the upper holder clamp screw, steadying the blade holder with the upper tool.

—*Kenneth Fletcher, Alexandria, Va.*

File card prevents tiny pieces from vanishing

When cutting out small, delicate parts on a scrollsaw, the miniscule results almost always fall through the table opening and into the debris below, requiring you to stop to search for them.

TIP: Make a cut in a 3×5" note card and tape it in place as shown below to keep those tiny cutouts on the table.

—*Floyd Bartling, Mount Aukum, Calif.*

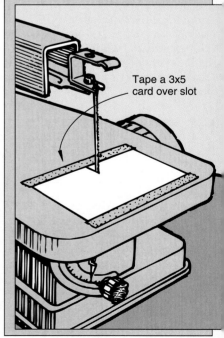

Tape a 3x5 card over slot

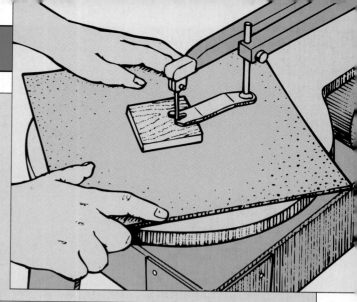

Cardboard protects fingers from blade

You're uncomfortable when your fingers come close to the blade while scrollsawing small parts.

TIP: Give yourself an extra margin of safety with a piece of cardboard (the back of a legal pad or the side of a cereal box will do the trick). Mount the workpiece securely at the center of the cardboard with double-faced tape or spots of hotmelt glue. Then, with the saw's holddown arm in place to keep the work against the table, guide your cut with your hands on the cardboard, a safe distance from the blade.

—*Alex Polakowski, Skokie, Ill.*

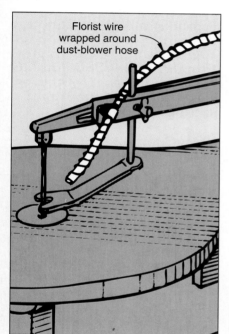

Florist wire wrapped around dust-blower hose

Florist's wire improves dust-blower arrangement

The plastic tubing from the dust-blower on some scrollsaws won't stay aimed at the cutting area.

TIP: Wrap the end of the tubing with florist's wire, the kind used to make artificial-flower stems or to arrange real flowers. (You also could use soft mechanic's wire or baling wire.) Space the wraps to make the tube look as if it has a spring wound around it. Now, you can bend the plastic tubing and aim it where you need to. The wire will help it stay put.

—*Carl Dachs, Englewood, Fla.*

Scrollsaw picks up dust instead of spreading it

Whenever you scrollsaw, the blower puffs a lot of sawdust onto you and into the air. You'd sure like to keep all of that messy dust under control.

TIP: Cut ⅛" plywood or hardboard to enclose the area beneath the saw table, and then bore a hole in it to accept a connector for the hose from your shop vacuum or dust collector. (Bore the hole in the existing sheet-metal cover, if your saw has one.) Be sure your modifications don't make it impossible for you to tilt the table and change the blade.

Drill a ½" hole into one side of the saw's hose connector, and epoxy-glue a 2" length of ½" (outside diameter) copper tubing into it. Slide the end of a piece of ½" (inside diameter) vacuum-line hose (you can find it at an auto-supply store) over the tubing. Route the hose around the saw throat to the hold-down foot. Now you have a double-duty dust collector for your scrollsaw, one that picks up dust at the blade and below the table.

—*Donald Diller, Coldwater, Ohio*

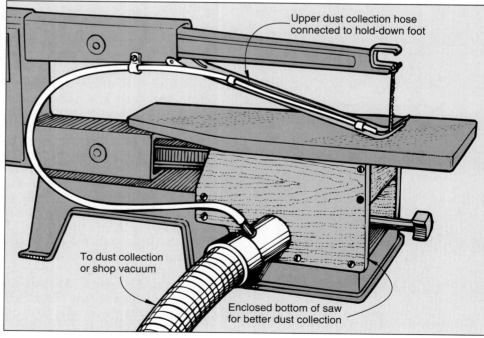

Upper dust collection hose connected to hold-down foot

To dust collection or shop vacuum

Enclosed bottom of saw for better dust collection

Tablesaws

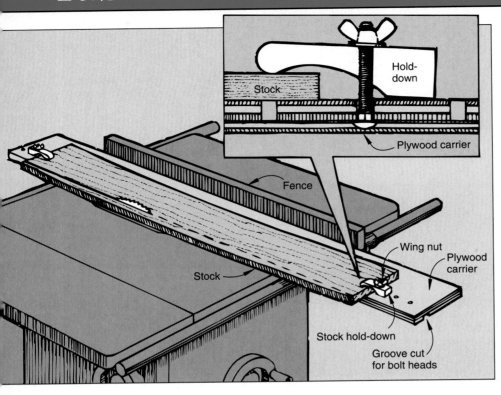

Hold-down

Stock

Plywood carrier

Fence

Wing nut

Plywood carrier

Stock

Stock hold-down

Groove cut for bolt heads

This jig quickly straightens edges

Attempting to rip a straight edge onto a board with irregular edges can be dangerous or downright impossible. One solution: Tack a straight board to the irregular board with finishing nails. Unfortunately, this method leaves small nail marks in the top surface of the workpiece.

TIP: Construct a carrier board from ¾" plywood to a width and length to accommodate most of your boards (14"×7' works for me). As shown at *left,* you can quickly clamp the workpiece to this carrier board, then rip one edge. Remove the workpiece from the carrier board, place the jig aside, and position the just-ripped edge along the fence to straighten the other edge.

—*Thomas Bruzan, Des Plaines, Ill.*

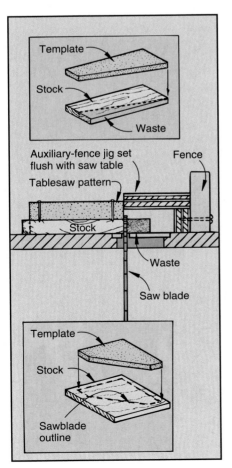

Template

Stock

Waste

Auxiliary-fence jig set flush with saw table

Fence

Tablesaw pattern

Stock

Waste

Saw blade

Template

Stock

Sawblade outline

Jig and templates duplicate irregular shapes

Sometimes, it seems almost impossible to safely and effectively cut several identical irregularly shaped pieces on a tablesaw.

TIP: A simple jig and custom-made templates help you cut tapers or nearly any irregular shape with straight sides. First, build an auxiliary-fence jig of ¾" plywood that allows plenty of clearance above and to the side of the saw blade as shown at *left.* The jig should be as long as the fence. Now, cut a template of the blank to be duplicated, taking extreme care to ensure correct dimensions and angles. Attach this to the workpiece with brads or double-faced tape, and rough-cut the wood material to within ½–1" of the final size. (A bandsaw works well for this task.) Then, with the jig attached to the fence, make the final cuts. For safety's sake, turn off the saw after each cut and clear the scraps to avoid possible kickbacks or binding.

——*Mike Jagielo, Almond, Wis.*

Brass screws solve sticky saw situation

Many shop-made tablesaw jigs employ hardwood strips that slide in the miter-gauge slots. But the strips sometimes swell and bind, or shrink and become so loose they affect accuracy.

TIP: Adjustable-width guide strips will end the problem. To make them, start with a hardwood strip slightly narrower (by ⅟₃₂" or so) than the width of the miter-gauge slot. Next, cut a ⅜"-wide notch ⅜" deep every 3–4" along one edge of each strip. (A ⅜" Forstner bit makes the notches quickly and accurately.) Center a pilot hole in each notch, and drive in a #6×½" round-head brass wood screw. (Don't use steel screws; they could cause the slots to wear excessively.) Now you can adjust the guide-strip for fit by turning the screws in or out.

—*Jerry Miller, Ringwood, N.J.*

Tablesaw jig chamfers small stock safely

You want to chamfer the corners of some small pieces of stock using the tablesaw. Your fingers end up uncomfortably close to the blade, though.

TIP: Construct the jig shown from ¼" plywood and scrapwood. Size the base according to the stock you'll be cutting and the distance between the saw's miter gauge and blade. Square one end to one side, and then attach cleats to the square corner with glue and brads. Be careful not to put metal fasteners into the cutting line. Clamp the jig to the miter gauge. Cut the corner off the jig, adjusting the position to achieve the desired angle on test stock. Then, cut your project parts safely and securely.

—Alan R. Holtz, Torrance, Calif.

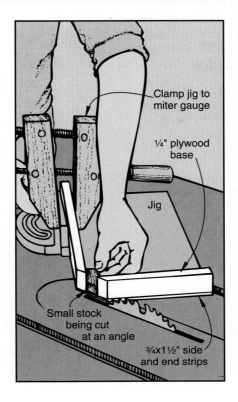

Clamp jig to miter gauge

¼" plywood base

Jig

Small stock being cut at an angle

¾x1½" side and end strips

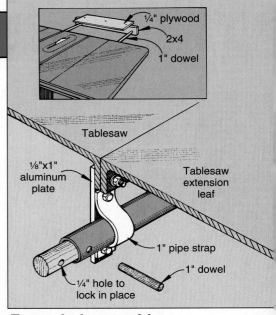

¼" plywood

2x4

1" dowel

Tablesaw

⅛"x1" aluminum plate

Tablesaw extension leaf

1" pipe strap

1" dowel

¼" hole to lock in place

Extended saw table catches cut-offs and supports long boards

Cut pieces fall off over the back edge of most saw tables because of the limited area behind the blade. Woodworkers sometimes reach across the blade to grab the piece–a dangerous thing to do.

TIP: Add a sliding extension to the back of your saw table. When pushed against the table edge, it will catch small pieces. Extended, it will support longer material.

To make one, start by cutting two pieces of plastic (or other) pipe long enough to extend from the front to the back of the table. Attach one to each side of the saw beneath the table with custom-built brackets. (See the drawing right.) Make sure that they don't interfere with the saw controls or limit blade tilt and elevation.

For the table, fasten plywood to a piece of 2×4 that's long enough to span the pipes, with an extra inch or so at each end. Then, cut two pipe-length dowels that fit snugly inside the pipes. Drill holes in the 2×4 to accept the dowels, glue the dowels into place, and slide the table into the pipes. To lock the table in position, drill through the pipe and into the dowel, and insert a ¼" dowel. For cutting heavy material, attach one or two legs to the back of the extension for extra support.

—Dave McFarlane, Fredericton, New Brunswick

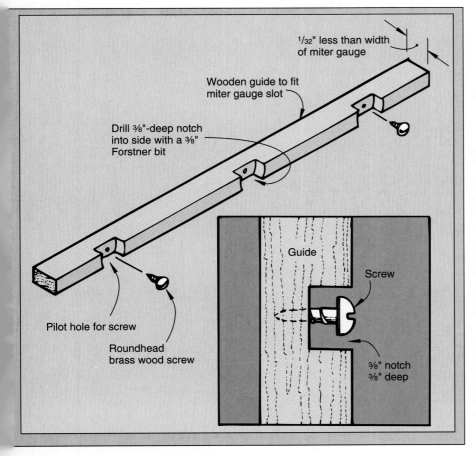

1/32" less than width of miter gauge

Wooden guide to fit miter gauge slot

Drill ⅜"-deep notch into side with a ⅜" Forstner bit

Pilot hole for screw

Roundhead brass wood screw

Guide

Screw

⅜" notch ⅜" deep

Tablesaws

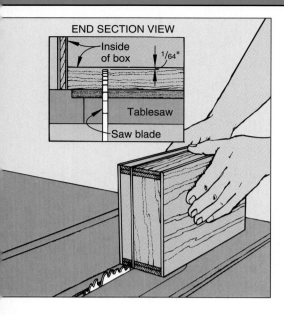

END SECTION VIEW

Inside of box

1/64"

Tablesaw

Saw blade

Sawing off a lid is easier if you don't quite cut it

When separating the lid from a small box using a tablesaw, the parts can pinch together, making things go haywire in a hurry.

TIP: Set your tablesaw's cutting depth about ¼" less than the thickness of your box sides and ends. Then, cut along the lid separation line as usual; the two parts will remain joined. Complete the job by cutting the lid free with a craft knife and sanding the edges of the lid and box.

—Arthur Conway, Biggera Waters, Queensland, Australia

Protect saw accessories from damaging falls

The miter gauge and rip fence on a tablesaw are delicate instruments designed specifically for assuring precise cuts. When cutting large pieces, you often have to remove one of these accessories. Unfortunately, both of them often find a home on the edge of a table from where they may fall to the floor, knocking them out of adjustment and jeopardizing your toes.

TIP: Install wooden holders for both the miter gauge and rip fence on the saw's stand. To make the miter gauge holder, simply cut a channel into a block to receive the bar on the gauge. For a retainer for the rip fence, add a side cleat of plywood to a length of wood slightly thicker than the fence and as long as the depth of the saw's base as illustrated in the drawing *below*.

—David M. Johnson, New Springfield, Ohio

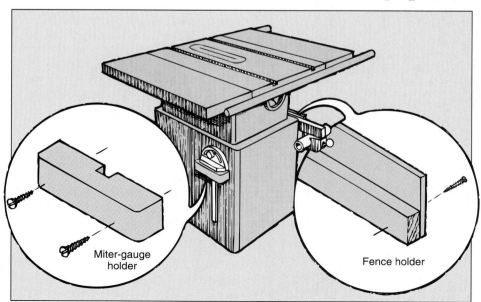

Miter-gauge holder

Fence holder

Crank it up, not down, when setting your saw

After cutting a series of dadoes with your tablesaw, you find some of them too shallow

TIP: Your tablesaw arbor moved down as you sawed, due to vibration and pressure on the blade. Guard against blade creep by following this procedure when you adjust blade depth: Lower the blade below your intended setting, and then raise it to the desired height. Don't lower the blade to the cutting height. If your saw has a locking knob on the height-adjustment crank, be sure it's tight before you start to saw.

--from the WOOD magazine shop

DOWN

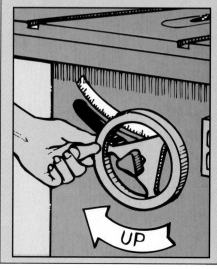

UP

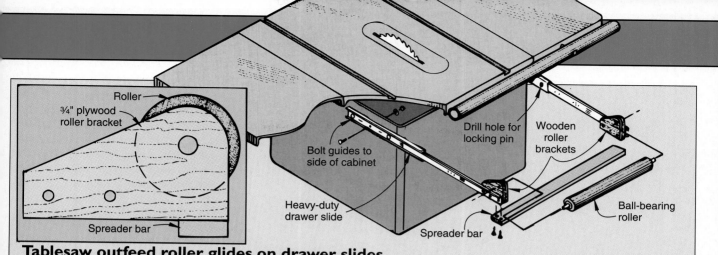

Roller
¾" plywood roller bracket
Spreader bar
Drill hole for locking pin
Bolt guides to side of cabinet
Wooden roller brackets
Heavy-duty drawer slide
Spreader bar
Ball-bearing roller

Tablesaw outfeed roller glides on drawer slides

You can't always find a helper when you want to rip long stock on your tablesaw. A floor-standing roller? That works great unless you have material stacked behind the saw or something else blocking the floor back there. There must be another answer.

TIP: Equip your tablesaw with a slide-away out-feed roller mounted on heavy-duty drawer slides. Choose side-mount slides that will extend far enough to place the ends about 36" behind the saw blade. Then, mount one slide on each side of the saw base, locating them so they don't interfere with the rip fence or the saw's controls or adjustments.

Now, screw a plywood bracket to the end of each slide, with the upper edges at table level or slightly below. Locate them to clear the rip fence when retracted. Add spacers as necessary to fit a standard outfeed roller (available from woodworking-supply dealers). Attach a spreader bar across the end for stability.

—*Ron Salmon, Kamloops, B.C.*

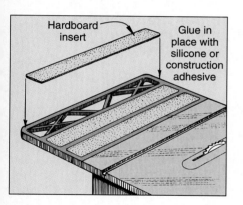

Hardboard insert
Glue in place with silicone or construction adhesive

Hardboard inserts neutralize finger-pinching extensions

Open-grid tablesaw extensions save a lot of weight and expense. The pain when you pinch your fingers between a board and a crossbar sometimes outweighs those advantages, though.

TIP: On extensions with a raised rim around the open gridwork, you can protect your fingers by covering the open areas with hardboard inserts. Select material thin enough that the insert surface will be lower than the metal table surface (¼" hardboard fits the Sears Craftsman saw illustrated). Measure the openings, and then cut a strip of hardboard for each. Sand or file the edges and corners as necessary for a snug fit, smooth side up. Glue the inserts into place with construction adhesive or silicone.

—*Robert Surman, Linden, N.J.*

Saw longer boards with assist from pipe clamps

A long, unsupported board end makes crosscutting on your table-saw tricky, as well as hazardous.

TIP: If your saw has tubular fence-guide rails, make a temporary table extension from two pipe clamps and a suitable board as shown at *right*. Align the top of the extension with the saw table, and position the clamp faces and handles safely out of the way before starting the saw.

—*Jim Moss, Fullerton, Calif.*

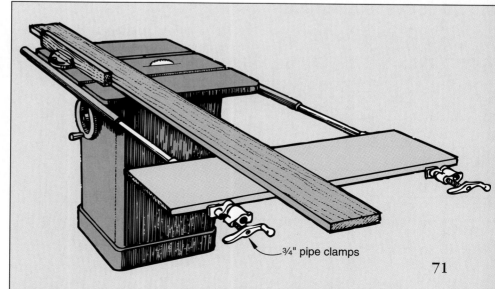

¾" pipe clamps

Tablesaws

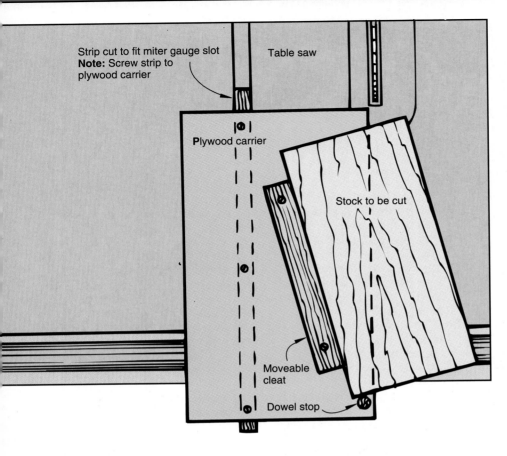

Strip cut to fit miter gauge slot
Note: Screw strip to plywood carrier

Table saw

Plywood carrier

Stock to be cut

Moveable cleat

Dowel stop

Carrier makes ripping at angles safe, easy

Making rip cuts at angles to the edge of a small workpiece can be both difficult and hazardous. Like many other shop tasks, a simple jig will make this operation much safer and easier.

TIP: Build an adjustable carrier using a 16×16" piece of ½" plywood. To the bottom side, screw a strip that snugly fits your saw's miter-gauge slot. Then, install a dowel stop near the rear edge as shown in the drawing at *left*. To the top side, screw a movable cleat, and reposition as needed to cut desired angles.

--Carl Cummings, Marcellus, Mich.

Stop blocks assure consistent dado cuts

Making identical dado cuts in a series of pieces can be tricky, particularly when the cut happens to be wider than the widest setting for your dado blade.

TIP: Measure carefully and clamp two separate blocks (A and B in the drawing *below*) to the top of your tablesaw to establish the right- and left-hand limits of the dado. Position the stock against stop block A, make the cut, and do likewise after aligning the stock with block B. Use scrap stock to check settings before cutting the actual workpieces, and hold the stock securely against the miter gauge.

—*Silvia Eder, Rio de Janeiro, Brazil*

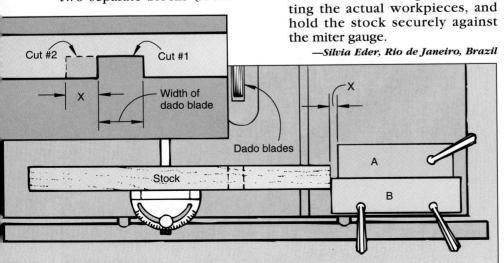

Cut #2   Cut #1

X   Width of dado blade

X

Dado blades

Stock

A

B

Set your fence accurately with this shop-made gauge

You can't rip accurately on your tablesaw unless you can set the fence parallel to the front and back of the blade. And some fences just seem to defy proper adjustment.

TIP: Set your fence more precisely with this easy-to-build jig. Construct the fixture shown at *right*, sizing part B to fit the miter-gauge slots on your tablesaw. Cut the notch through part B so that the bottom lies flush with the saw table when part B sits in the miter-gauge slot. Match the width of the notch to a wooden yardstick or ruler.

Slide the ruler or yardstick into the completed fixture. With part B in the miter-gauge slot and the fence in position, slide the ruler over until the end touches the rip fence. Tighten the thumb-screw (the dowel inside the fixture will clamp the ruler tightly without denting it). Move the jig fore and aft to gauge the slot-to-fence distance at other points.

—*Rinaldo Edward, Allen Park, Mich.*

Altered carriage bolt fits saw table to a T

Fiddling with clamps to secure jigs and feather boards to your tablesaw eats up shop time. And sometimes the clamps don't hold very well anyhow. There must be a better way.

TIP: You can bolt your tablesaw helpers right to the saw table if it has a T-shaped miter-gauge groove. Grind the head of a ½×2½" carriage bolt to fit the groove, as shown *right*. Cut a ½" slot in the feather board (or other attachment) to allow adjustment, install it over the bolt, and secure with a flat washer and wing nut.

—*Jim Bloomfield, Saugus, Calif.*

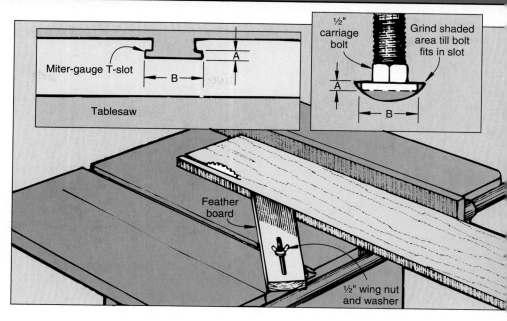

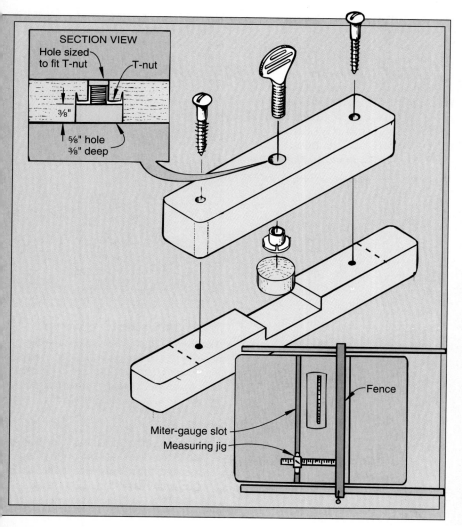

Locking pliers hold saw blade in a pinch

Wedging a tablesaw blade with scrapwood when loosening (or tightening) the arbor nut doesn't always hold the blade immobile.

TIP: Clamp your locking pliers onto the blade near the rim, positioning the jaws to clear the teeth. Brace the pliers against the table. Now when you apply the wrench to the arbor nut, you won't lose your hold, or skin your fingers, on the blade.

—*Jim Prelesnik, Renton, Wash.*

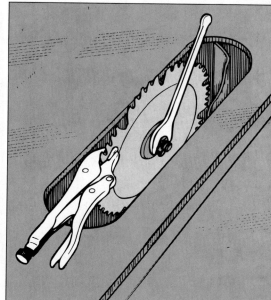

Tool Maintenance

Sandpaper cleaner works on stones

While touching up the edges on your cutting tools, you notice that metal filings have clogged your stone. Is there some quick way to clean the stone?

TIP: Wipe the sharpening stone dry, and then clean it with the same rubber cleaning stick you use on your sanding belts and discs. Rub the cleaning block hard on the stone several times to remove sharpening residue.

—*John Hillestad, Lynden, Wash.*

Dial 0 on dial indicator to align jointer tables

Even a slight misalignment between your jointer's infeed and outfeed tables can result in a noticeable error after several passes. You need a way to adjust that infeed table accurately.

TIP: Use a level, a dial indicator, and a clamp to align your jointer's adjustable infeed table with the fixed outfeed table quickly and precisely. Lay the level on the outfeed table along one side. Then, clamp the dial indicator (available from hardware or auto-supply dealers) to the end of the level, setting the indicator to 0 at one corner of the infeed table.

Now, position the indicator probe on another corner of the infeed table by moving the level. Press the level firmly to the outfeed table. Adjust the infeed table to bring the dial reading to 0, if necessary. Similarly adjust the other corners, and recheck.

—*John Platania, Loveland, Ohio*

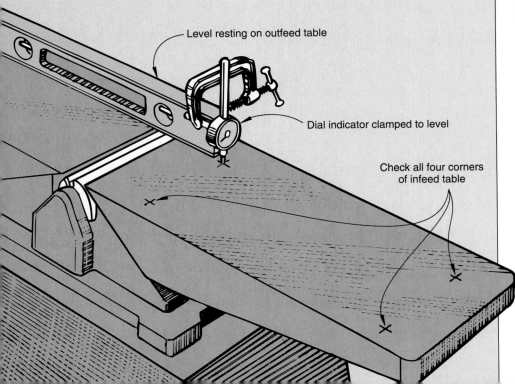

Level resting on outfeed table

Dial indicator clamped to level

Check all four corners of infeed table

Wooden wheels with tires replace tired-out casters

Hard-plastic caster wheels on some machine bases crack or break up after a while. Replacing the entire caster can be costly if you have several that need your attention.

TIP: Don't replace the entire caster, just the wheel. Remove the original wheel by grinding the staked end of the caster axle. Make the new one from scrap hardwood. To cut the wheel, set your hole-cutter radius to that of the original wheel minus the thickness of your tire material. (Strips cut from inner tubes work great.) Glue the tire to the wheel with cyanoacrylate adhesive, fastening the ends with tacks. Use a bolt of appropriate diameter and length as an axle, enlarging the hole-cutter pilot-bit hole to fit.

—*Larry McConnell, Medford, Ore.*

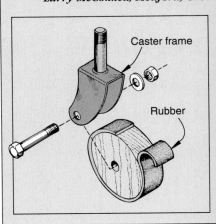

Caster frame

Rubber

Vise takes hold to help loosen circular saw blade

You just can't keep the blade from turning as you try to loosen the tightened arbor bolt or nut on your portable circular saw.

TIP: Place the saw on your bench vise, and clamp the blade in the jaws. Now, you can loosen that stubborn bolt with the blade held in a firm grip.

—*Ed Smigowski, Comins, Mich.*

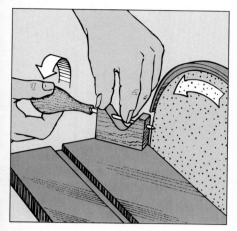

Get right to the point when sharpening an awl

When sharpening an awl (or a center punch), it's all too easy to make the tip look more like a faceted diamond than a smooth, pointed cone.

TIP: Form a perfect tip with this jig made from 1½×1½×2" scrapwood. To make one, drill a hole ¹⁄₆₄" larger than the tool's shaft diameter lengthwise through the stock. Bandsaw or scrollsaw the opening shown. Glue non-skid material onto the bottom.

To use, insert the tool, set the jig at the proper angle to a belt or disc sander, and rotate the tip against the moving abrasive, holding the jig with your other hand. Maintain drag by pressing a finger against the tool shaft.

—*Jay Wallace, Ashland, Ore.*

Make a clean sweep when seeking tool parts

Repair parts for some imported power tools can be tough to find or make yourself.

TIP: Don't overlook any possible source for substitute parts. Vacuum cleaner and sewing machine dealers carry a variety of drive belts, for instance. A wide, flat one could replace a damaged tire on a small bandsaw. A sewing-machine drive belt might fit a power tool with a broken belt.

—*Patricia Knute, Lake Worth, Fla.*

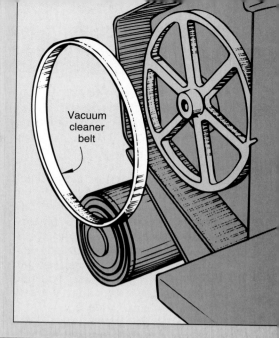

Modified blade makes carving knife better

The thick, wide blade on your new carving knife is unwieldy in tight areas.

TIP: Grind the sides and tip of the blade as shown at *right* on a slow-speed water wheel or grinding stone. While you're thinning the blade, round over the top edges, too. The reground blade will still be plenty strong for carving and a whole lot easier to use.

—*Harley Refsal, Decorah, Iowa*

Tubing keeps chisel edges from going down the tubes

When you have to store chisels in a drawer or toolbox with other tools, the sharp edges often get chipped and dulled. They'll still be sharp enough to gash your fingers when you reach in there, though.

TIP: Slip some plastic tubing from the hardware store onto those blades, extending it past the edge. Pick tubing that fits the blade snugly. Now, your edges and your fingers will be safer.

—*Kenneth Rewinkel, Sunnyvale, Calif.*

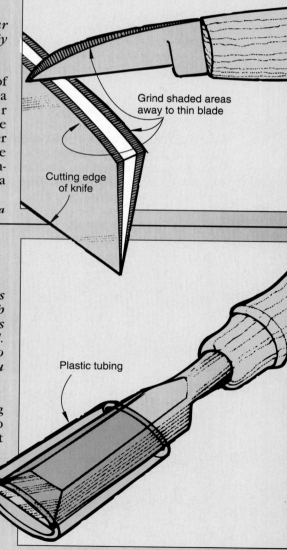

Tool Maintenance

Brassy solution for a sloppy miter gauge

Your miter gauge fits loosely into the table slot. This side play affects the accuracy of your cuts.

TIP: Put your miter gauge back into the groove with a snug-fitting guide bar. First, measure the amount of play with feeler gauges, available from auto-supply stores. Slip different gauges into the gap between the miter-gauge bar and the side of the slot until you find one that minimizes play yet still allows the bar to slide.

Then, from brass stock of that thickness, cut a strip to fit the side of the bar. (Buy thin brass shim stock from a hobby shop or auto-supply dealer.) Bond it to the side of the bar with cyanoacrylate adhesive. Polish and wax the bar.

—Mel Morabito, Mahopac, N.Y.

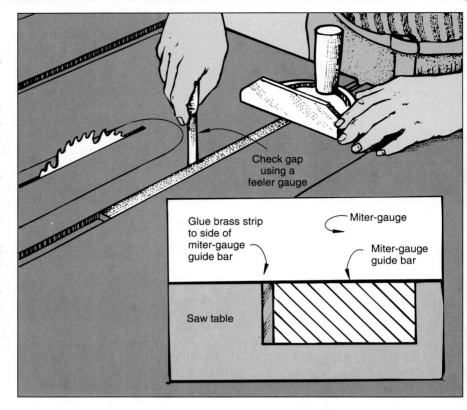

Check gap using a feeler gauge

Glue brass strip to side of miter-gauge guide bar

Miter-gauge

Miter-gauge guide bar

Saw table

Slide to side eases nicked-knife grief

AARGH! A ridge on the board! Something has nicked your thickness-planer or jointer knives. You have a few more pieces to plane, no spare knives, and the sharpening shop is closed for the weekend. Are you just out of luck?

TIP: You can still complete that project. Move one of the knives 1/16" or so to one side, and carry on with the job. By offsetting the nicks on the blades, your stock comes out clean.

—Gary Miller, Peek, Minn.

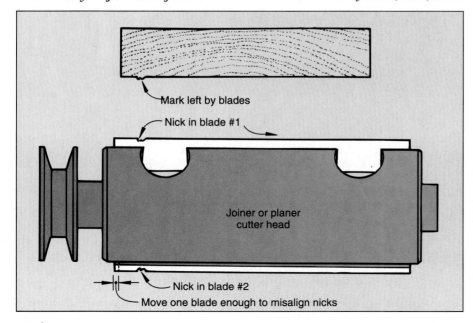

Mark left by blades

Nick in blade #1

Joiner or planer cutter head

Nick in blade #2

Move one blade enough to misalign nicks

Scrapwood wrench turns troublesome thumbscrews

Sometimes, you just can't grip a thumbscrew firmly enough to tighten or loosen it. Plus, you can't get the leverage you need.

TIP: Scrollsaw a slot large enough to fit over the thumbscrew in the center of a piece of 3/8" to 3/4"-thick scrapwood about 1 1/2×4". Round the corners and edges of this wooden wrench with a file, and drill a hanging hole in one end.

—John Seidel, Smyrna, Ga.

Turning

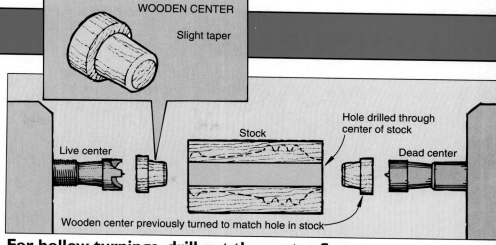

WOODEN CENTER

Slight taper

Live center

Stock

Hole drilled through center of stock

Dead center

Wooden center previously turned to match hole in stock

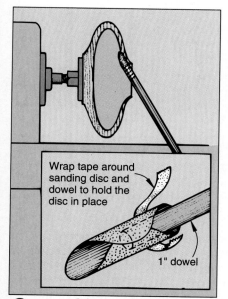

Wrap tape around sanding disc and dowel to hold the disc in place

1" dowel

Carry a big stick to sand turnings

There are times when you just can't get your hand inside a turned bowl or vase on your lathe for sanding. And sometimes it may be too dangerous to try sanding by hand—when you're turning distressed wood, for instance.

TIP: Reach into that turning with a sanding stick made from a 1×36" dowel and a sanding disc. Wrap the sanding disc (any size from 3" to 6" will work) around the dowel with about 1½" of it extending past one end. Secure the disc with masking tape. With the dowel against the tool rest, insert the sanding disc into the vessel in the 2–4 o'clock area.

—*Marc Wroe, Tempe, Ariz.*

For hollow turnings, drill out the center first

Some pieces such as salt-and-pepper shakers, or slide-action grips for antique firearms, require large holes in the center of circular pieces of stock. Boring the holes after turning the workpiece can be troublesome if you can't easily hold onto it. And, it's nearly impossible to bore the hole in the exact center.

TIP: Start by boring the desired hole in the square stock. Then, turn slightly tapered wooden centers, as shown *above*, that insert into the stock and allow secure mounting to the lathe.

—*James R. Watts, Robinson, Ill.*

Marked handles aid in turning-tool selection

It's convenient to lay turning tools under the lathe bed while working. If the handles all look the same, though, it's difficult to pick up the right tool when you can't see the cutting tips.

TIP: Color-code each handle with a paint stripe. Mark gouges, for instance, with red, and skews with blue. Mark the size on each one (or draw a profile of the tip) with a black marker. Now, when you reach for a tool, you'll be sure to get the right one.

—*William White, Williston, Vt.*

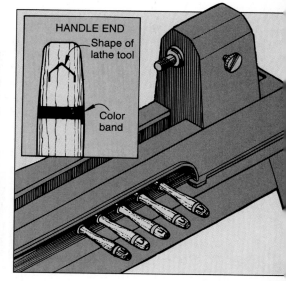

HANDLE END

Shape of lathe tool

Color band

Economy chuck for turning small-diameter stock

If you only occasionally need a small-lathe chuck, owning one can be an expensive luxury. Here's a way to make one for just a couple of bucks.

Spindle

Weld two nuts together for a chuck

TIP: Welding two 1" nuts (8 TPI) together makes a great economy chuck for Delta or Rockwell lathes. (For other brands, check the thread size before purchasing the nuts.) First, turn the blank between centers, tapering one end of the stock from 15/16" to 13/16" as shown at *left*. Then, screw the chuck halfway onto the lathe spindle, and screw the tapered end of the workpiece into the available threads of the combined nuts. Now, you can turn a thimble or other small projects.

13/16" diameter

15/16" diameter

—*Frank Lynn, Kelso, Wash.*

Turning

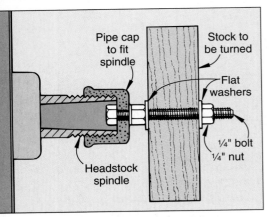

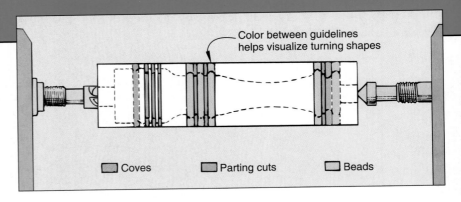

Color between guidelines helps visualize turning shapes

☐ Coves ☐ Parting cuts ☐ Beads

Pipe-cap lathe arbor holds wheels for turning

You'd like to turn grooves around some wheel blanks so they look like tire treads. How can you mount those discs on your lathe?

TIP: Mount an iron pipe cap on your lathe spindle, to make a simple arbor to hold the discs. With the cap on the spindle and the lathe running, file the closed end of the cap flat. Then, drill a hole the same size as the disc center hole (¼" in our example) through the center of the cap. Insert a bolt of appropriate length and diameter from inside the cap, and fasten it with a nut. Then, slide a flat washer, the wheel blank, and another washer onto the bolt, securing them with a nut.

—Bob Thompson, Harrisburg, Penn.

Color-coded turning minimizes mistakes

As soon as you start the lathe, your carefully laid out pencil marks for a spindle turning become a confusing whirl. It's all too easy to turn a cove where you wanted a bead.

TIP: To avoid confusion, code your turning with colored pencils (not markers—they'll soak into the wood). Lay out the turning as usual. Then, shade the sections between the lines with colors to represent different cuts—for instance, yellow for coves, and green for beads. Now, with the lathe running, the color stripes will guide you through the turning. Buy colored pencils at art-supply or stationery stores.

—Chuck Caranna, Columbus, Ohio

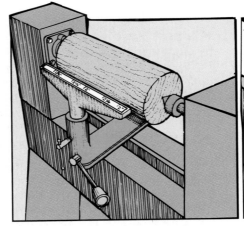

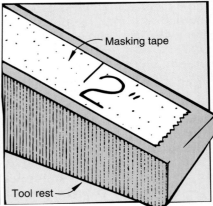

Masking tape

Tool rest

Tape records diameters for woodturning layout

Constantly referring to templates on small turning projects slows things down, but you do need to know diameters at various reference points.

TIP: When you set up your lathe for a turning, put a strip of masking tape along the top of the lathe tool rest. Mark the reference points and diameters onto it. Now, you have a handy guide to those turning diameters that's right where you need it whenever you need it.

—Glen Plum, Riverside, Calif.

To turn a taper, plane a flat spot

Turning a straight taper on a table or chair leg tests any woodworker's patience. It seems there's no easy way to do it.

TIP: Give yourself a guideline to follow. Establish the major and minor diameters with a parting tool. Then, plane a straight taper between them, using the longest hand plane available. Check the tapered flat spot with a straight-edge. When you start the lathe, you'll see a phantom guideline that you can follow right on up to a perfectly turned taper.

—From the WOOD magazine shop

Plane taper

Major diameter   Turning square   Minor diameter

Workbenches

Pipe clamps provide basis of a hefty end vise

You want to add an end vise to your workbench but there just isn't room in your tool budget.

TIP: Fashion your own end vise from some lumber and a pair of ¾" pipe clamps. Bore holes through the bench end for the clamps, as shown *below*. Install blocking as needed to transfer clamping forces to the sliding clamp jaw instead of the workbench supports. Add a 1×4 for the fixed jaw at the end of the bench, and then construct the laminated movable jaw shown. The butterfly openings allow the jaw to swivel to accommodate objects having nonparallel sides.

—Floyd Jines, Baton rouge, La.

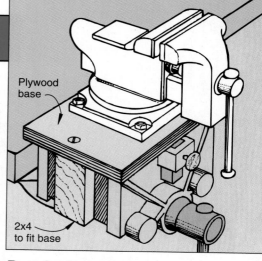

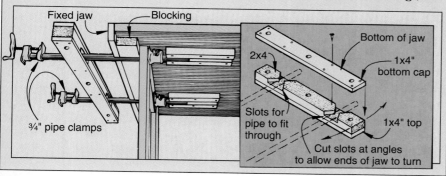

Bench vise stays scarce until you need it

A mechanic's bench vise often comes in handy, but it isn't very handy to have it taking up most of a corner of the bench.

TIP: Mount the vise on a base that clamps into your woodworking vise. Cut a piece of ¾" plywood as long as your woodworking vise's jaws, and about 1" wider than the width of the mechanic's vise. Mark and drill the plywood for ⅜ or ½" T-nuts or threaded inserts (depending on the vise's mounting-bolt size). Cut a piece of 2×4 to fit lengthwise along the center of the bottom of the plywood. Fasten the narrow edge of the 2×4 against the plywood with screws and glue. Bolt the mechanic's vise to the base. Store the vise out of the way. Then, when you need the mechanic's vise, just secure the base in your woodworker's vise.

—Alan Holtz, Torrance, Calif.

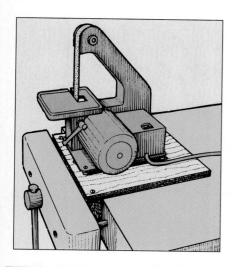

The virtue of a vise: taming benchtop tools

You have so many benchtop tools now that you can't fit them all on top of your bench. You can store them somewhere else, but how do you keep a tool solidly in place when it's time to use it?

TIP: Cut a ¾" plywood base for each tool and fasten a 2×4" cleat to the front edge. Store them out of the way. When you're ready to use one, place it on the bench and clamp the cleat in the vise.

—John Hogsett, Beaver, Pa.

Bench extension reaches out to meet project needs

A regular-length (5' or 6') workbench is fine for most jobs. Sometimes, though, a longer one is handy, especially when you're working with sheet materials or long boards.

TIP: Build a sliding extension for your bench. Construct it as shown at *right* from plywood and 2×4s or adapt it to match your bench design. Make the sliding panel so it will be flush with the benchtop when closed. For a heavy-duty extension, add a provision for auxiliary legs on the slider.

—Bill Selkirk, Plattsburgh, N.Y.

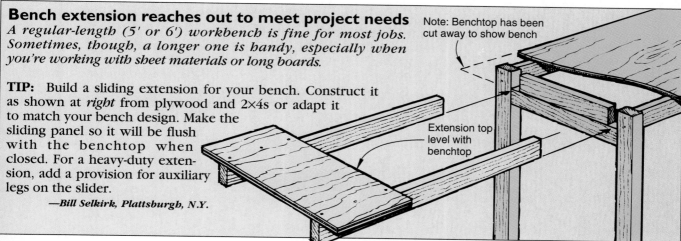

Note: Benchtop has been cut away to show bench

Extension top level with benchtop

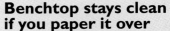

Dowel

H

Auxiliary backsplash
Backsplash

2"

Same as dimension H in detail drawing

Bench stop

This bench stop eliminates need for benchtop holes

For planing, carving, and lots of other tasks, bench dogs are a big help. But what if you don't want to drill holes in your benchtop?

TIP: Equip your workbench with a bench-stop system that uses a series of holes along the backsplash. First, make the stop from a piece of 1½×3" hardwood that's long enough to reach from the backsplash to the front edge of

your workbench. Center a ½" hole about 1½" deep on one end. Glue in a dowel pin, letting ½–¾" extend from the stop. Now drill a row of ½" holes on 2" centers ¾" from the bottom edge of an auxiliary backsplash, and screw it onto the existing one.

To use, just insert the dowel into one of the backsplash holes and clamp the stop to the bench.

—F. Eldon Heighway, Phoenix, Ariz.

Grinder on stilts lies low between uses

Though you don't use your bench grinder often, it's bolted to the workbench, taking up valuable space. Why? Because otherwise, it wanders all over the benchtop whenever you turn it on.

TIP: Unbolt the grinder from the bench, and then insert the mounting bolts back into the holes on the machine base. Run the nuts right up to the bottom of the base, and tighten them. Now, you can store the grinder, which looks like it's standing on threaded stilts, out of the way.

When you need to use it, just place it on the benchtop, letting the bolts extend into the holes. To reduce vibration, slide a rubber washer onto each bolt before setting the grinder into place.

—Homer A. Bruno, Palmyra, N.J.

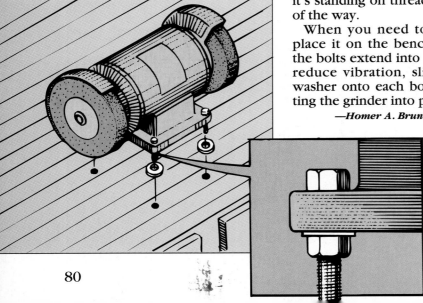

Benchtop stays clean if you paper it over

You try to keep your benchtop clean. but gluing, painting, staining, varnishing, and other tasks invariably end up leaving puddles or stains behind, marring that spotless surface.

TIP: A roll of masking paper from the paint store will keep that benchtop tidy. Hang the roll with a simple holder at one end of your bench. Tear strips off and lay them on the bench before you start a messy job. Paint and glue and other goo won't soak through, so when you're done, cleanup is as easy as throwing out the paper. Masking paper comes in several sizes–we found 12"×60 yd. to be convenient.

—from the WOOD magazine shop

The rabbet habit makes your vise more versatile

Your workpiece rocks up and down and keeps falling out of the vise whenever you try to work on the face. You need a better grip.

TIP: When you make jaw liner for your vise, cut a ⅜×⅜" rabbe along the top inside edge of each liner as shown at *right*. Install the liners flush with the benchtop. The rabbeted edge lets you clamp firmly while keeping the face above the bench and vise.

—Bob Colpetzer, Clinton, Tenn

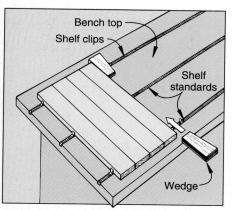

Bench top
Shelf clips
Shelf standards
Wedge

Shelf supports hold boards on bench, too

Wedging a workpiece between adjustable bench stops makes sanding and other operations easier. But laying out and drilling holes for the stops is slow work.

TIP: Rout grooves, as shown *above*, instead of drilling holes. Install 4'-long steel shelf standards into routed grooves in your benchtop, setting the faces of the standards slightly below the surface. Space them 9–12" apart, or far enough apart to meet your requirements. Then, just place shelf clips as necessary, securing the workpiece with wooden wedges. (You also could position the clips to work as stops with your vise.) Remember to apply force to the top of the shelf clips.

—*Roger Sauerbrunn, Dongola, Ill.*

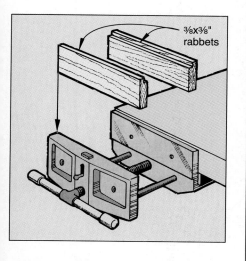

³⁄₈x³⁄₈" rabbets

Keep cord in suspense for fewer surprises

While belt-sanding a project piece on top of your workbench, you lurch to a stop when the sander cord snags on the bench edge. That problem fixed, you start again, but almost run over the cord with the sander.

TIP: Get that cord out of the way with a few stout rubber bands. Loop them together to form a chain about three feet shorter than the distance from your shop ceiling to the benchtop. Screw a hook into the ceiling above the center of your workbench, and hang your rubber-band chain from it. Now, when you plug in a tool, pass the cord through the bottom rubber band first. Position the tool's cord so it stays off the bench.

—*Dan Walters, Merritt Island, Fla.*

Router mat flips out for more convenience

Your non-slip router mat sure comes in handy. But, when you roll it up to put away, you end up with a bulky bundle that can be hard to store.

TIP: Hang the mat out of the way over an end of your workbench. Place the mat near one corner, fold it over the end of the benchtop, and fasten it with aluminum carpet edging or countertop molding. When you don't need the mat, simply flip it over the end of the bench.

—*Chuck Hedlund, Des Moines, Iowa*

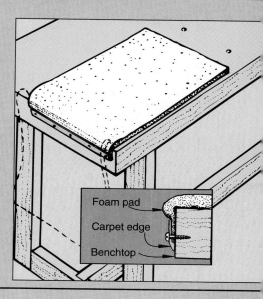

Foam pad
Carpet edge
Benchtop

Hole in bench handy for cutting and cleaning

You dread cutting with your sabersaw because of the balancing acts needed to hold the stock over the edge of your bench.

TIP: Cut a hole in your workbench top like the one shown at *right*. Reinforce it with cleats and place a box under the opening. When you have some cutting to do, place your stock with the cutting line over the opening and saw away. The box will catch much of the sawdust, and when you sweep the benchtop, just brush the rest through the hole. Save the cutout, and drill a 1"-diameter hole in it for a finger grip. Replace the insert when you need a full benchtop.

—*C. A. Conway, Benton City, Wash.*

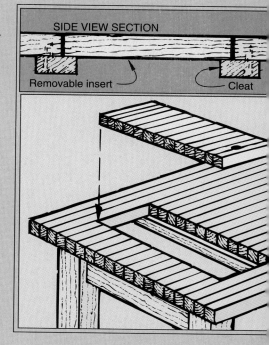

SIDE VIEW SECTION
Removable insert
Cleat

Miscellaneous

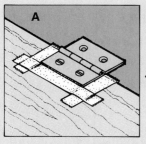 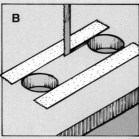 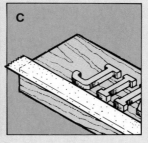

Making the most of versatile masking tape

If you only use masking tape for routing painting tasks, you've just scratched the surface of potential applications.

TIP: As shown in the three examples *above*, you can use masking tape for many marking and align- ment tasks. Here, we lay out the position of a hinge, mark the cutting lines for a slot after drilling the two end holes, and align letters on a wood surface. Unlike pencil marks, the mask- ing tape lifts off easily.

—*From the* **WOOD** *magazine shop*

A little heat loosens stubborn rusty screws

Badly rusted woodscrews are tough to remove from old furni- ture, boats, or any other wooden product. Using brute force often accomplishes little other than roughening up the screw slot and marring the wood surface, and raising your blood pressure.

TIP: Heat the head of the screw with a hot soldering iron for a few minutes. That should loosen the fastener enough so you can remove it easily. This method also helps you remove screws held in place with epoxies and other strong adhesives.

—*Michael A. Yahn, Jamestown, N.Y.*

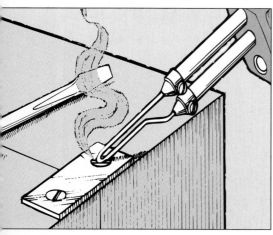

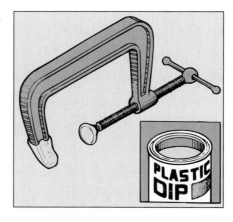

Plastic dip works great on other end of tools, too

There are all sorts of ways to pro- tect wood from clamps. Unfortunately, most would be easier to accomplish if you had three hands.

TIP: Coat the business end of your clamps with the plastic-dip material marketed to coat tool handles. It dries to a soft, flexible coating that will protect even fin- ished wood. Apply it by dipping or brushing, taking care to keep it out of movable joints or threads. Coat the grip end of a pair of pli- ers or locking pliers, too, to make a handy tool for pulling out wood- en axle pegs and the like.

—*Raymond Babcock, San Angelo, Texas*

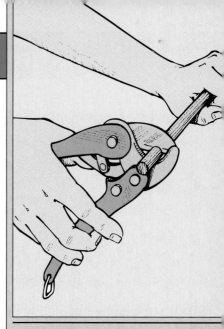

Old glove finger protects carver's thumb

As careful as you are, it's all too easy to gash your thumb while carving. Wearing a glove is just too clumsy, though.

TIP: Don't wear the entire glove, just a part of it. Cut the fingers from an old leather glove before you throw it away. Then, just slip one onto your thumb whenever you carve. Always endeavor, of course, to keep your thumb and fingers out of harm's way.

—*Maurice Anderson, Denver, Colo.*

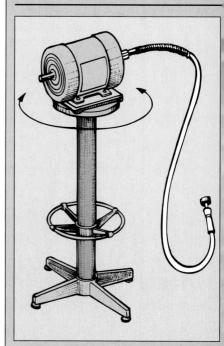

PVC cutter makes short work of short dowels

Setting up jigs to cut short lengths of dowels takes time. Wouldn't it be great to just snip off those little rounds?

TIP: Drop by a plumbing-supply shop, and buy a PVC pipe cutter—the squeeze-handle type. With a razor-sharp blade and a ratchet mechanism with high mechanical advantage, this tool clips cleanly through dowels up to ½" diameter with little effort. A good one with metal handles will cut dowels for a long time to come.

—Charles Simpson, Guntersville, Ala.

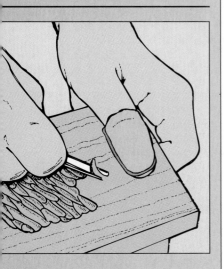

Motor for flexible shaft swivels on barstool stand

Mounting the electric motor for your flexible-shaft tool on the workbench isn't always convenient.. You may need to move the motor to avoid kinking the shaft as you manipulate the handpiece.

TIP: Perch the motor on a stand made from an old swivel barstool. Replace the seat with ¾" plywood, and then mount the motor to the plywood. Add weight to the bottom of the stool for stability, if necessary. Now, you can place the floor-standing motor wherever you need it in your shop. What's more, the motor will swivel easily to follow the shaft.

—Gene Krietemeyer, Columbus Grove, Ohio

Widening the gap for screwdriver blade

You need a screwdriver slot in a piece of hardware. Unfortunately, a hacksaw cut is going to be too narrow for the screwdriver blade.

TIP: Make a wider slot by putting two blades in the hacksaw frame when you make the cut. If you need a really wide slot, try adding another blade to the stack.

—James Lee, Lawrenceburg, Tenn.

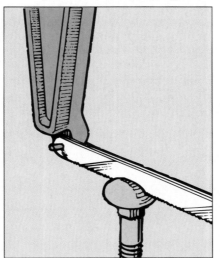

A two-wheel deal easily hauls heavy sheet goods

You've already clobbered two corners and an edge of a 4×8' sheet of ¾" plywood while trying to maneuver it through your shop. And you hate to think about what you've done to your back. Isn't there a better way to handle big, heavy sheets?

TIP: Roll those unwieldy goods around on a two-wheel dolly like the one shown *below*. Cut the body pieces to the sizes shown from 1¹⁄₁₆"-thick maple or other hardwood. Cut the dadoes in the base. Then, cut out the axle block and drill the ½" hole through it as shown. Now assemble the sides, base, and axle block with screws and glue. Insert the axle in the hole, and slip on the wheels, securing them with axle caps. (Hardware stores sell the parts.) To use, stand the sheet material on edge, and raise one end off the floor. Slide the dolly under the end, and move it toward the middle of the sheet. Then, balancing the sheet on the dolly, roll it where you need to go.

—WOOD magazine's IDEA SHOP

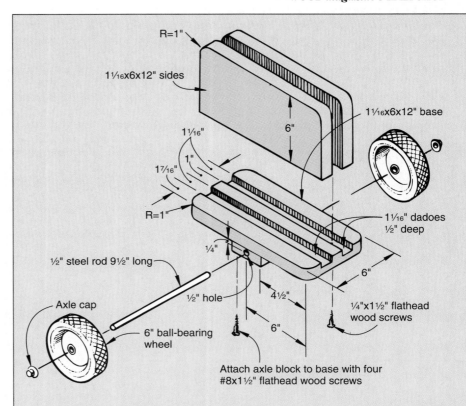

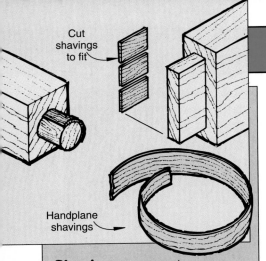

Cut shavings to fit

Handplane shavings

Shavings correct loose-fitting joints

Little things can happen to produce tenon joints or dowel holes that don't have the snug fit necessary for a strong joint.

TIP: Rather than trashing the undersized member, cut some thin shavings from a scrap piece of the material with a hand plane. Glue these thin shavings to the tenons or dowels and sand to fit.

—*David A. Alexander, Oneonta, N.Y.*

Add an apron to lap tray for easy-chair carving

Sometimes it would be nice to plunk down in the living room and relax, but you hate to give up that carving time. You could carve while you're sitting there, but you'd draw flak for scattering chips all over the sofa and carpet.

TIP: Build a lap tray from scrap lumber and plywood, and then stitch up a canvas or denim apron. Arrange the apron as shown below, and then staple the hem to your lap tray. Now, you're ready to carve in comfort.

—*John Blyth, Wadsworth, Ohio*

Temporary feet lift project above harm's way

Before a project reaches completion, it can suffer a lot of dents and dings in the shop. Cabinets or bookcases built of plywood often end up with chipped face veneer at the bottom from being shoved around on the shop floor.

TIP: Attach scrapwood blocks to the bottom corners of your project with finishing nails or small screws. Leave the temporary feet on until you've finished the project and moved it to its final location.

—*from the* WOOD *magazine shop*

Framing-square gauges mark mitersaw stops

Most mitersaws have stops at common angles so you can switch from left to right cuts quickly. Making cuts at some other angle isn't quite so easy, though, without a reliable stop.

TIP: On some saws, you can mark your angle with a pair of stair gauges, the type that hardware stores sell to clamp onto a framing square. To use them, swing your saw to the desired angle to the right, and then install a gauge on the saw's front apron. Repeat for the left side. Now, you can swing the saw from angle to angle quickly and accurately without measuring.

—*James Marsh, USN*

More comfortable handle isn't just a pipe dream

Adjustable cranks on some woodworking machines have fixed handles. They get the job done, but when you need to change your setups often, those handles can raise a few blisters.

TIP: Take the friction out of adjustment by making a rotating handle from plastic pipe. Cut a length of PVC pipe to fit over the crank handle (½" pipe fit the drill-press table crank shown *below*). Drill and tap the end of the metal crank handle for a 10-32 machine screw. Then, drill a ³⁄₁₆" hole through the center of a wooden disc or PVC pipe cap. Slide the length of pipe onto the handle, and secure the disc or cap with a screw and washer.

—*William King, Marion, Iowa*

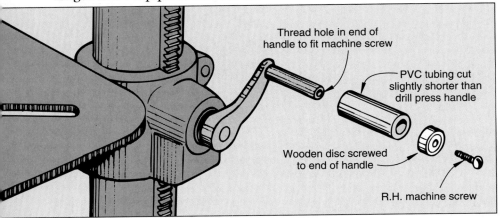

Thread hole in end of handle to fit machine screw

PVC tubing cut slightly shorter than drill press handle

Wooden disc screwed to end of handle

R.H. machine screw

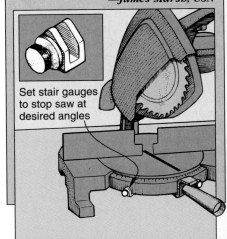

Set stair gauges to stop saw at desired angles

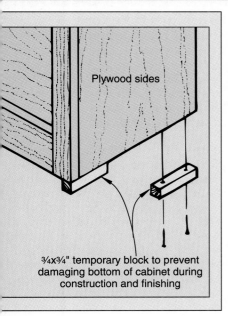

Plywood sides

¾x¾" temporary block to prevent damaging bottom of cabinet during construction and finishing

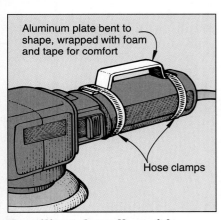

Aluminum plate bent to shape, wrapped with foam and tape for comfort

Hose clamps

Auxiliary handles aid arthritic woodworker

Arthritis makes it increasingly difficult for you to grip some of your power tools, but you don't even want to think about giving up the pleasure of woodworking.

TIP: An additional handle can help you hang onto many tools such as the sander shown *above*. Form the handle from 1–1½" aluminum strap stock ⅛" thick, and attach it to the tool housing with hose clamps or other appropriate hardware. Do not drill holes or insert screws into tool housings without consulting a tool-service professional. Wrap the new handle with plastic foam and tape for more comfort.

—Wayne Pepper, Janesville, Wis.

Dowel springs to action for easier spindle repair

Sometimes you can glue a broken chair spindle back together, with a dowel for reinforcement, but you'd like to do the job without taking the entire chair apart.

TIP: A spring and a dowel can save the day. First, remove the broken spindle. If it can be saved, modify it as shown in the drawing, at *right*. If it is beyond help, make a two-part replacement with the joint shown. Test before assembly. With the dowel, a strong spring, and the paper clip in place, glue and reinsert the lower spindle section. Next, glue and reinsert the top spindle piece and glue the dowel joint. Align both spindle parts, and then pull out the paper clip. The spring will force the dowel into place, making a strong joint.

—Walter Kalinowski, Elizabeth, N.J.

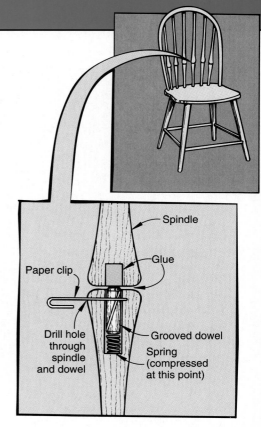

Spindle

Glue

Paper clip

Drill hole through spindle and dowel

Grooved dowel

Spring (compressed at this point)

Masking-tape shortcut makes short cuts easier

You're working on a project which calls for a number of same-sized short dowels, but measuring and marking them for cutting is seriously slowing your pace.

TIP: Measuring from the blade, mark the desired length on the saw table with a piece of masking tape. Line up the end of your dowel with the guiding edge of the tape and make your cuts.

—From the WOOD magazine shop

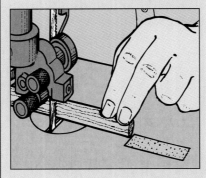

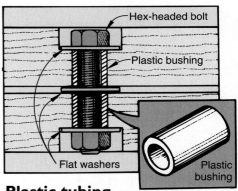

Hex-headed bolt

Plastic bushing

Flat washers

Plastic bushing

Plastic tubing makes pivot points sturdy

An easy way to make a pivot or hinge (as for a folding lawn chair) is to drill through the pieces and fasten them with a bolt and nut. But metal wears the wood down, leaving a sloppy fit.

TIP: Separate the wood and the metal with plastic tubing. Select tubing that fits the bolt snugly. Then, drill through the wooden pieces to fit the tubing outside diameter. Cut a length of tubing as a bushing for each wooden part, and assemble as shown below.

—Bob Kettler, Cincinnati, Ohio

Miscellaneous

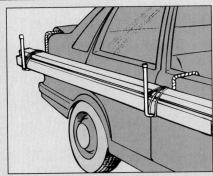

Lugging lumber home is easier with pipe racks

It's downright dangerous to drive around with boards sticking out through the windows of your car Hauling lumber inside puts a lot of wear and tear on your car's upholstery, too.

TIP: Solder short lengths of ¾" rigid copper plumbing pipe together with 90° elbows, tee fittings, and caps to make a pair of handy, portable yokes like those shown *above* for your car or truck. With measurements from your vehicle, size the yokes so the load sits level just below the windowsills and rear-view mirror on the passenger side.

Wrap the hooks that hang over

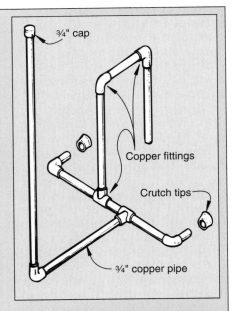

¾" cap

Copper fittings

Crutch tips

¾" copper pipe

the door or fender with plastic tape or foam pipe insulation to protect the car's paint and interior. Put crutch tips or padded scrapwood on the ends that rest against the car body. (Make the ends broad enough to prevent denting the car when the carriers are loaded.) Tie the load securely to both yokes, and take care not to overload the rack.

—*Paul Matulewicz, Blackwood, N.J.*

Bushings take toys out of bush league

A wooden wheel mounted on a wooden toy with a screw or bolt eventually becomes wobbly as the metal axle wears the center hole to an ever-larger egg shape. The wheel could even split.

TIP: Keep those wheels turning with fewer problems by incorporating bushings into the wheels. Simply select a piece of brass or copper tubing that fits snugly but freely over your axle screw or bolt. Size the axle hole in the wheel so the tubing fits into it tightly. Press a piece of tubing about ¹⁄₁₆" longer than the wheel thickness into the axle hole. (To prevent the tubing from getting a kink in it, place the screw or bolt into the tubing as you press it in.) Secure the bushing by flaring the ends with a center punch.

—*Howard K. Gaston, Naples, Fla.*

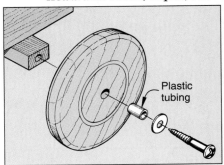

Plastic tubing

Get a better grip when machining dowels

It's hard to hang on to small dowels for cutting. Even with a V-block, you can lose control of those small cylindrical pieces.

TIP: Make a holder that grips dowels firmly. Start by drilling a line of dowel-sized holes through a piece of ¾×¾" scrapwood about 6" long. On an adjacent face, drill and countersink holes for two 10-24×1¼" flathead machine screws.

Then, rip the piece along the centerline of the dowel holes. Insert the machine screws through the countersunk holes in the bottom piece, install the top piece, and thread a wing nut on each screw. To hold a dowel, just loosen the wing nuts, slide the dowel through the appropriate hole, and tighten the nuts.

—*Frank Graham, Dartmouth, N.S., Canada*

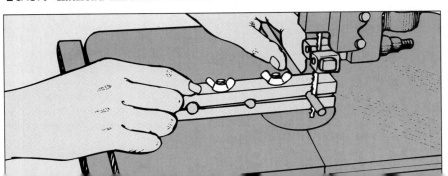

Drilled can cap prevents spray straw from straying

You need to squirt some spray lubricant into a tight spot, but you've lost that little red straw,

TIP: When you do find the elusive spray tube, simply drill through the plastic can cap with a drill bit the same diameter as the straw. (A ⁵⁄₆₄" hole made a tight fit for the tubes in our shop.) Then, stow the straw by sticking it through the cap; it always will be right there with the can when you need it.

—*Robert N. Anderson, Fairfax, Vt.*

Hearing yourself keeps extended projects on track

Often you'll start a project and not be able to get back into the shop for several days. By then, you may not remember where you were in the job.

TIP: Add a hand-held cassette tape recorder—the kind used for business memos—to your shop equipment. Then, talk to it about your project. Talk about steps you have completed or have left to do, machine setups, dimensions, and, things you need to check. Start the taping for each workshop session by announcing the date. (Reset the tape counter to 0, too).

Now if you're away from the shop for a few days, just rewind the tape to the beginning of the notes made the previous time and listen as your recorded comments bring you right up to date. Store the recorder in a resealable plastic bag to protect it from sawdust.

—Dan Wilks, Gowrie, Iowa

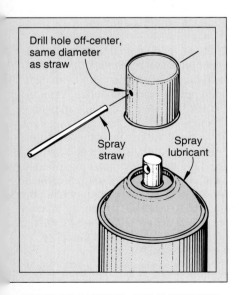

Drill hole off-center, same diameter as straw

Spray straw

Spray lubricant

An economical buffer

A drill-mounted buffing wheel can perform all sorts of work-shop polishing chores. But, at about $10 apiece, the cost of several wheels really adds up.

TIP: Cut a paint-roller tube into lengths to fit over a 1½" sanding drum (thick naps work best). Slip these fuzzy tubes onto the drum and polish away.

—Mark D. Hoover, Poway, Calif.

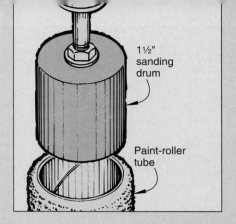

1½" sanding drum

Paint-roller tube

Paper mask prevents fogged-up glasses

You should wear a particle mask when you're making sawdust , but the masks cause your glasses to fog up.

TIP: Disposable paper masks, from medical supply stores, work just fine with glasses. They have a thin strip of metal to conform to your nose and elastic bands to hold the mask to your face.

—Judy Coffey, Elk Grove, Calif.

Pipe insulation protects projects from damage

Your sawhorses mar project parts and you're just not having much luck keeping shop rags in place on the sawhorse edges.

TIP: Open up a piece of formed foam insulation for ¾" pipe and slip it over the sawhorse. It grips well enough to stay in place, and protects sanded parts from damage.

—R.J. Cooke, Newington, Conn.

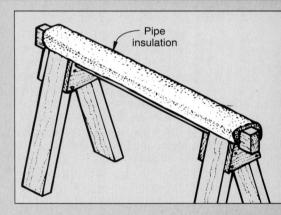

Pipe insulation

Screwdriver stretches allen wrench's reach

Sometimes, you can't quite reach an allen-head screw with one of those little L-shaped wrenches. And there are those times when the wrench will reach, but you can't get a firm enough grip on it to make it turn.

TIP: Get an old screwdriver and drill a hole in the blade to fit the allen wrench. Put the short end of the wrench through and secure it with a rubber band. Now, you can reach into that tight spot, with the screwdriver handle providing a solid grip.

—David Blake, Huntington, W. Va.

Rubber band

Allen wrench

Screwdriver

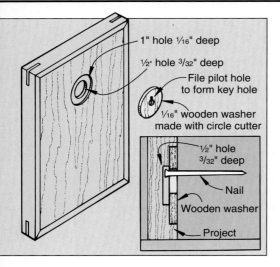

- 1" hole ⅟₁₆" deep
- ½" hole ³⁄₃₂" deep
- File pilot hole to form key hole
- ⅟₁₆" wooden washer made with circle cutter
- ½" hole ³⁄₃₂" deep
- Nail
- Wooden washer
- Project

Thin-stock hanging slot drilled instead of routed

A keyhole hanging slot routed into the back of a wall-mount project sure makes it easy to build and hang up. But, if you're working with thin stock, you're out of luck.

TIP: Try this procedure to make a keyhole hanging slot in stock as thin as ³⁄₁₆". All you need are two Forstner bits and a circle cutter. First, using the circle cutter, cut a 1"-diameter disc from material about ⅟₁₆" thick. Then, elongate one side of the pilot-bit hole with a file, forming a keyhole shape.

Next, bore into the back of the project with a 1" Forstner bit to a depth equal to the thickness of the disc you just made. In the center of that hole, bore ⅟₁₆–³⁄₃₂" deep with a ½" Forstner bit. Now, glue the disc into the 1" counterbore, pointing the elongated portion of the center hole up.

After the glue dries, you're ready to hang the item over an appropriate screw or nail. The void left by drilling with the ½" bit will allow room for the fastener head behind the hanging slot.

—James Upham, Midland, Tex.

Handle saves hands from allen wrench

Those L-shaped allen wrenches really dig into your hand during repeated use—when you're threading a lot of inside cuts on certain scrollsaws, for instance.

TIP: For relief, add a comfortable hardwood handle to the wrench. Along one edge of ¾×1×12" stock, saw a groove the width of the allen wrench (⅛" in the instance shown) and about ½" deep. Round over the edges of the stock by sanding or routing. Then, cut the handle to length, taking into account the size of your hand and any obstructions the handle will have to clear when in use. Drill a hole through the bottom of the slot, and epoxy the wrench into place in the wooden handle.

—David Weber, Latrobe, Pa.

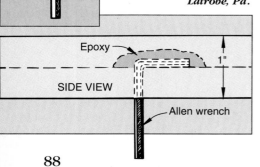

END VIEW

Epoxy

SIDE VIEW

1"

Allen wrench

Stair-tread safety material makes better tire treads

What can you do about toy wheels that skid on smooth surfaces and mar floors?

TIP: Buy a roll of self-adhesive non-skid rubber—the thin, gray safety tread with a surface that looks something like a sponge. Cut the roll into ½"-sections the width of the wheels you're making. When you turn the wheels, form a groove to fit the tread, about ⅟₃₂" deep around the circumference of each. Cut a strip of tread long enough to fit into the groove. Apply contact cement inside the groove and allow it to dry before laying the tread in place. With rubber treads, your wheels will skid less, scar less, and last longer.

—Johnny Janssen, Anaheim Hills, Calif.

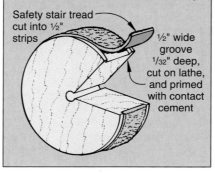

Safety stair tread cut into ½" strips

½" wide groove ⅟₃₂" deep, cut on lathe, and primed with contact cement

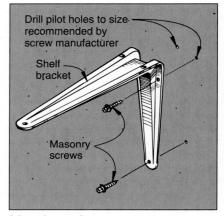

Drill pilot holes to size recommended by screw manufacturer

Shelf bracket

Masonry screws

Hardened screws overcome concrete-wall hang-ups

You need some more shelves and cabinets to organize your shop. But you dread the struggle that goes with attaching them to concrete or block walls.

TIP: Don't install anchors and drive screws in order to secure shop paraphernalia to concrete walls and floors. Rather, eliminate the middle step by using masonry screws. These hardened screws drive right into a pilot hole drilled with a masonry bit, thus eliminating the need for lead or plastic wall anchors. When using masonry screws, be sure to pay careful attention to the manufacturer's recommendations concerning pilot-hole depth and diameter, as well as load capacity.

—WOOD magazine's IDEA SHOP

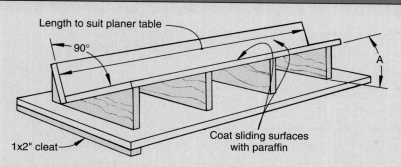

Length to suit planer table

90°

A

1x2" cleat

Coat sliding surfaces with paraffin

Clamp at front and back

Auxiliary table

Workpiece

Planer makes bevels a saw can't handle

Sometimes, you want to cut a bevel that your tablesaw or jointer just can't handle, such as beveling the full width of a long piece of 8"-wide stock.

TIP: Do the job with your planer, employing an auxiliary table made from scrapwood and ply-

wood like the one shown *above*. Make it long enough to reach from the front edge of the planer's infeed table to the back edge of the outfeed table. Cut angle A accurately; it determines the bevel angle. Sand the sliding surfaces smooth and coat them with paraffin wax. Clamp the fixture to the

planer table. Scribe a reference line for the bevel on the end of your workpiece, then lay it on the angled surface of the auxiliary table. Feed it through the planer, taking a series of shallow cuts to shave a perfect bevel on the face.

—*Todd Grieser, Archbold, Ohio*

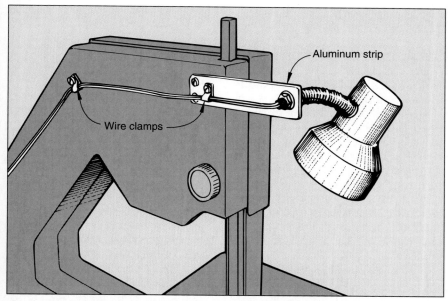

Aluminum strip

Wire clamps

Spotlight your work with a reading lamp

No matter how well-lit your shop, nothing beats a tool-mounted work light for seeing what's going on. They're pretty expensive, though, so lighting up several tools could be hard on the wallet.

TIP: An adjustable reading lamp—the type made to clamp onto a bed headboard—costs less and works great. After removing the plastic clip from the threaded tube on the lamp, attach the lamp

to a custom-made bracket. When you mount it to the tool, make sure that the lamp, the bracket, the cord, and the mounting hardware don't interfere with tool or create a safety hazard.

Hardware and variety stores, and home centers sell the lamps. Also, don't toss out that clip you removed. It serves a number of needs around the shop, from clamping to holding plans.

—*Roger Jewell, St. Joseph, Mich.*

This straightedge helps you rout and rip accurately

A straightedge aids ripping or routing a large sheet of plywood but it takes time to adjust the straightedge so the blade or bit cuts exactly on your layout line.

TIP: Make a smarter straightedge by gluing a 2"-wide strip of ½"-thick stock to an equally long piece of ¼" plywood or tempered hardboard. Both pieces should be a few inches longer than your longest cuts, and the ¼" piece should be wider than the distance from your saw's blade (or router's straight bit) to the edge of the tool's base. When the glue dries, rip or rout the ¼" stock as shown *below*. Now, you can align this just-cut edge with your layout mark and know where the cut will start.

—*Roger Boulet, Winnipeg, Manitoba*

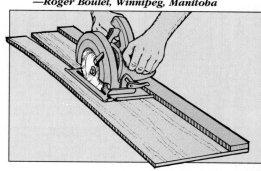

Miscellaneous

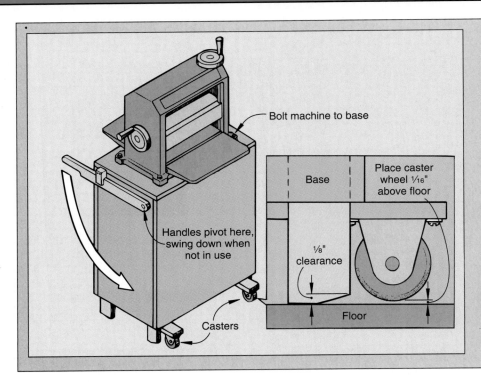

Bolt machine to base

Handles pivot here, swing down when not in use

Casters

Base

Place caster wheel 1/16" above floor

1/8" clearance

Floor

Make your tools into wheelbarrows

Putting your tools on wheels allows you to get the most out of your shop space. But, putting all of that equipment on mobile bases would cost a fortune.

TIP: Mount a pair of 2"-diameter rigid-plate casters behind the rear legs of the tool or stand, placing the wheels about 1/16" above the floor. Then, install a wheelbarrow-style handle on each side of the tool as shown at *left*

Now, just lift the handles to move your tools wheelbarrow style. As a bonus, the equipment sits solidly on its legs whenever it's in use---you don't need to chock or lock the wheels.

—Jim Skey, Malvern, Pa.

Threaded inserts go straight with simple installation jig

Methods for driving threaded inserts often rely on a drill press for accuracy. What do you do when your workpiece is too big for the drill press?

TIP: Put together a jig like the one shown *below*: Drill a centered 1/4" hole (or one that fits a bolt that threads into the inserts you're using) 3/4" from one end of a 3/4×2×5" piece of wood. Glue that piece on top of a 3/4×3×4" block, forming a lapped T. Insert a 1/4×2½" hex-headed bolt through the hole, and put a nut on it.

Now, screw the threaded insert onto the bolt about 3/8" and run the nut down to jam the insert. Hold the jig against the workpiece with the insert over its hole, and turn the hex-head of the bolt with a wrench to drive the insert in. When the insert is in place, hold the bolt head with one wrench and back off the jam nut with another.

—Paul R. Cook, Westfield, N.Y.

Hex-head bolt

Nut to lock threaded insert to bolt

Hole in stock to fit insert

Benchtop equipment doesn't have to be on the bench

With benchtop space at a premium, permanently mounting power tools is out of the question. Here's a quick, solid, temporary mounting.

TIP: Turn your tablesaw into a tool stand. First, cut a 3/4"-thick auxiliary base for the tool. On the underside, attach a strip that fits your saw's miter-gauge groove Then, rabbet one edge of another piece of 3/4" stock, forming a lip that fits between the table edge and rip-fence guide rail. Attach this positioner to the front edge of the auxiliary base, perpendicular to the miter-gauge strip, rabbet facing out. Now mount the tool.

To set up, place the auxiliary base on the saw table (the miter-gauge strip locates it). Secure it with a wedge between the edge of the table and the backside of the positioner.

—Al Eichman, Hilton Head Island, S.C.

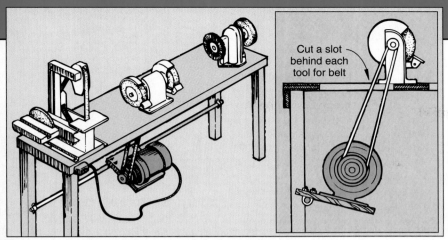

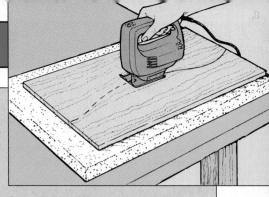

Put a grinding halt to multiple motor costs

A motor adds mightily to the cost of benchtop power tools such as grinders, buffers, and strip sanders. Since you can't use more than one of these machines at once, it's a shame to tie up a lot of money in a motor for each individual machine.

TIP: You can mount these benchtop tools alongside each other and run them with one motor that slides from tool to tool as shown *above*. Fasten a ½–1 hp motor to a length of ¾" pipe with eye- or U-bolts and a plywood base. Add a step-down pulley to the motor and a switch along the front of the bench. Cut holes into the bench top for the belts to run through.

—*Dennis Baer, Fayetteville, Ga.*

Hardboard cleans up portable saw's cuts

Rather than wrestle a big sheet of plywood across your tablesaw, you decide to cut it with a portable circular saw. The only problem: a splintered edge.

TIP: For splinter-free sawing, equip your portable saw with a zero-clearance base. Cut a piece of ¼" tempered hardboard to fit your saw's sole plate. Raise the blade, and fasten the hardboard to the sole plate with countersunk flathead machine screws and nuts.

Next, clamp the saw to a sawhorse, keeping the area below the blade clear. Plug the saw in, turn it on, and slowly lower the blade through the hardboard to make the zero-clearance blade slot. Turn the motor off and then mark where the blade guard hits the hardboard. Use a jigsaw or coping saw to cut out a slot that allows the blade guard to return to its down position. When using a portable saw, cut with the good face of your material down.

—*Jon Grasson, Olney, Md.*

Insulation keeps you cool when cutting with a sabersaw

You're getting steamed trying to make an intricate cut with your portable sabersaw. There just doesn't seem to be any way to support the workpiece firmly.

TIP: A piece of 2"-thick Styrofoam insulation board will cool you down. Lay it on the floor or workbench, with your workpiece on top. Now, saw away! Your workpiece won't slip around, and it will be supported on both sides of the cutting line. A standard-length sabersaw blade won't cut all the way through the 2" foam board so you can cut even thin materials. The insulation board will last a long time before it needs replacing.

—*Pierre Duval, Quebec, Canada*

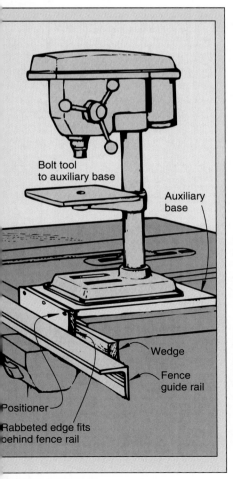

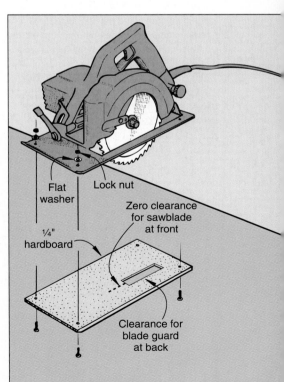

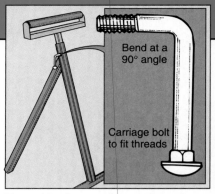

Bend at a 90° angle

Carriage bolt to fit threads

Struttin' your stuff for smoother planing

Many planers have infeed and outfeed tables that provide little support for long stock. Extension tables help, but you need to level them with the planer tables

TIP: You can minimize chances of snipe by building hinged extension tables such as the one shown *below*.

Flatten the pipe ends with a hammer. Once assembled, adjust the pitch of the extension table by turning the ¼" nuts. With a level, or long straightedge, check carefully to make sure the planer table and extension table form a single flat plane.

—John Patton, St. Louis.

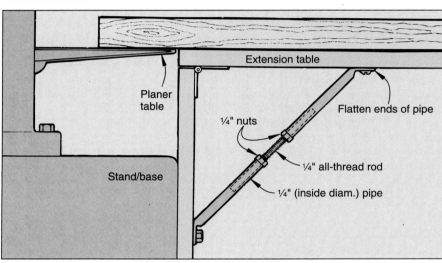

Extension table

Planer table

¼" nuts

Flatten ends of pipe

¼" all-thread rod

¼" (inside diam.) pipe

Stand/base

Bent bolt replaces knob for easier adjustments

You'd feel more comfortable if you could tighten an adjustment a little more, but you can't grip the knob well enough to screw it down any tighter. You need something with a bit more leverage.

TIP: Replace setscrew-type knobs with a lever to make tightening a cinch. Buy a bolt of the same diameter and thread as the adjustment knob and about 6" long (or use threaded rod). Clamp it in your vise (be careful not to damage the threads), and bend a right angle in the bolt, leaving a straight, threaded end at least as long as the threaded portion of the original knob. With the bent bolt screwed into the threaded hole, you'll have the leverage you need to secure that adjustment.

—Stan Schwartz, Bothell, Wash.

Panels won't defeat you if you deck them first

Wrestling sheet goods around in a small shop wears you out fast. And trying to place sawhorses so you can cut a panel without assistance adds another dimension to your irritation.

TIP: If you have an outdoor deck and it's a nice day, don't even mess with those sheets or sawhorses inside your shop. Lay the material flat on the deck, placing the cutting line over a

space between decking planks. Adjust your portable circular saw to cut a little deeper than the material thickness. Now, you can cut the sheet safely and easily. As a bonus, you'll have less sawdust to sweep up in your shop, too.

—Janet A. Collins, East Bridgewater, Mass.

Bigger knobs enable easier adjustments

Sometimes, you just can't grip a small adjustment knob firmly enough to turn it, Pliers will batter it up in no time, particularly a knob you adjust frequently, such as the scrollsaw blade tensioner shown right.

TIP: Cut a disk from ¾" scrapwood with your holesaw (a 2"-diameter one works well). Round over the edges for comfort and safety. Bore (or scrollsaw if the knob isn't round) a hole in the center to fit tightly over the troublesome knob, and then glue the big gripper in place with epoxy.

An easy way to reverse patterns

Some methods of transferring a pattern to a work surface, such as ironing a photocopied pattern as described in a shop tip in the February 1990 issue of WOOD magazine, result in a reversed image. Since a reversed image will not always work, there ought to be a way to re-reverse the pattern you want to use.

TIP: Photocopy the pattern or lettering you want onto an acetate transparency. You can purchase these transparencies at an office- or art-supply store, or have an instant printing shop do the job for you. Photocopying the transparency onto a sheet of paper as shown *below* will give you a reversed pattern.

—*Ed Zieverink, Cincinnati*

For even heftier knobs, use thicker stock. Or, add style by starting with laminated discs.

—*Bob Thompson, Harrisburg, Pa.*

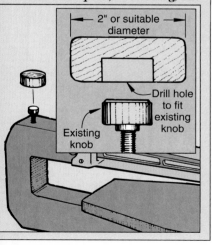

Take dowel gauge along to head off workshop woes

You've just bought half a dozen ½" dowels. But, a couple of them are too big, and one measures more like ⁷/₁₆".

TIP: Since dowel sizes aren't precise, it pays to check them out before you buy. How? Just take a dowel gauge when you go shopping for those often irregular rods.

Make a simple gauge from a piece of scrap plywood. Drill and label a hole for each size dowel you ordinarily use, along with holes ¹/₁₆" larger and smaller than those sizes. The gauge will help you select dowels to fit holes you've already drilled. It also will help you select a bit to drill holes to fit dowels you have on hand.

—*Alex Chalmers, Myrtle Beach, S.C.*

Pattern of protection

Ragged outlines begin to appear on a pattern after just a few tracings. And, if you have to stop in the middle of the job, you can lose track of the spot where you left off.

TIP: To get extra mileage from your patterns, place a sheet of waxed paper over them before getting started. You'll not only protect the pattern, but you can quickly tell what you've traced, and what you haven't.

—*Reuel Smith, Halifax, Nova Scotia*

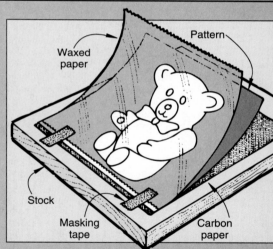

Waxed paper · Pattern · Stock · Masking tape · Carbon paper

Dab of hotmelt glue steadies rocking shelves

After carefully positioning four shelf standards inside a cabinet, you install the clips and put in the shelves. But the shelves still rock.

TIP: Place a drop of hotmelt glue on top of the shelf support that's too low. Set the shelf into place as the glue cools, and hold it level so that the glue forms a leveling pad on the support. Use this trick on wooden, plastic, or metal shelf supports. It works with glass shelves, too.

—*Steven Caron, Aberdeen, S.D.*

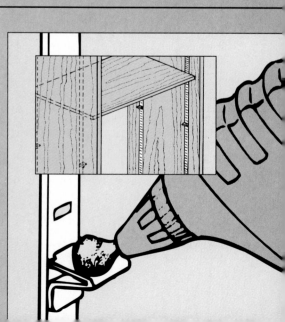

Index

Better Homes and Gardens® WOOD® PLANS™

ALL-TIME FAVORITE PROJECTS FROM THE EDITORS OF WOOD® MAGAZINE

ORDER YOUR FAVORITE PLAN TODAY!
1-800-572-9350

BUILDING-BLOCK CASTLE PLAN
TS-1006 $9.95

PARTY-TIME CART PLAN
OFS-1004 $9.95

COMFY COUNTRY TRIO PLAN
OFS-1012 $9.95

THREE-OF-A-KIND SOUTHWEST TABLE PLANS
IFS-1005 $9.95

3 QUILT HANGER PLANS
IFS-1008 $9.95

QUILT RACK PLAN
IFS-1004 $9.95

HEIRLOOM CHEST PLAN
IFS-1009 $9.95

MAHOGANY TABLE AND CHAIR PLANS
Table OFS-1006 $9.95
Chairs OFS-1007 $9.95
BUY BOTH PLANS FOR $14.00

ADIRONDACK FURNITURE PLANS
LAWN CHAIR ....OFS-1001 ....$9.95
SIDE TABLE AND
FOOTSTOOL.....................OFS-1014............$9.95
ROCKER ....OFS-1016......... $12.95

AMERICANA COLLECTION PLANS
DA-1002 $12.95

OAK DRY SINK PLAN
IFS-1002 $9.95

CHIPPENDALE WALL MIRROR PLAN
IFS-1006 $9.95

TWO-PART PATIO CHAIR PLAN
OFS-1020 $9.95

SHOP TESTED

ORDER TODAY!
CALL 1-800-572-9350

7:00 AM - 4:30 PM CST. VISA and MasterCard accepted.
Please fill out order form before placing order.

Name_____
Address_____
City_____ State _____ ZIP _____
Payment: _____ Check _____ Money Order _____Visa _____MC
Credit Card #_____exp. _____
Signature_____

STOCK #	QTY.	PLAN NAME	PRICE EA.	TOTAL

LESS SPECIAL DISCOUNT (IF APPLICABLE): $
TOTAL ORDER: $

TO ORDER: Send your name, address, and the name of the plan(s) you wish to receive, plus a check or money order (U.S.) for each plan. Postage and handling plus state and local taxes, if applicable, are included. Allow 4-6 weeks for delivery. **Mail to:**

WOOD Magazine Plans
P.O. Box 9255, Dept. WD-ST-1
Des Moines, IA 50306

100% money-back guarantee if not completely satisfied.